THE ENCYCLOPEDIA OF
NORTH AMERICAN ARCHITECTURE

THE ENCYCLOPEDIA OF
NORTH AMERICAN
ARCHITECTURE

Janice Anderson

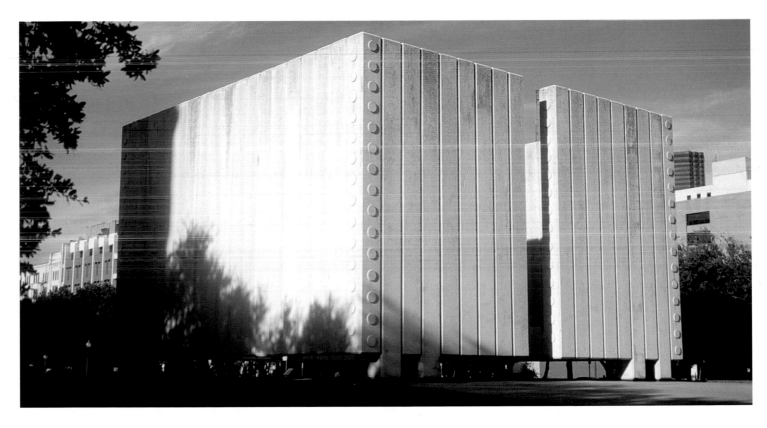

CHARTWELL
BOOKS, INC.

Published in 2006 by
Regency House Publishing Limited
Niall House
24–26 Boulton Road
Stevenage, Hertfordshire
SG1 4QX, UK

**Copyright © 2006 Regency
House Publishing Limited**

For all editorial enquiries please
contact
Regency House Publishing at
www.regencyhousepublishing.com

ISBN-13: 978-0-7858-2091-8
ISBN-10: 0-7858-2091-4

Printed in China

In memory of
Neil Grant
Writer and Historian
(1938–2005)

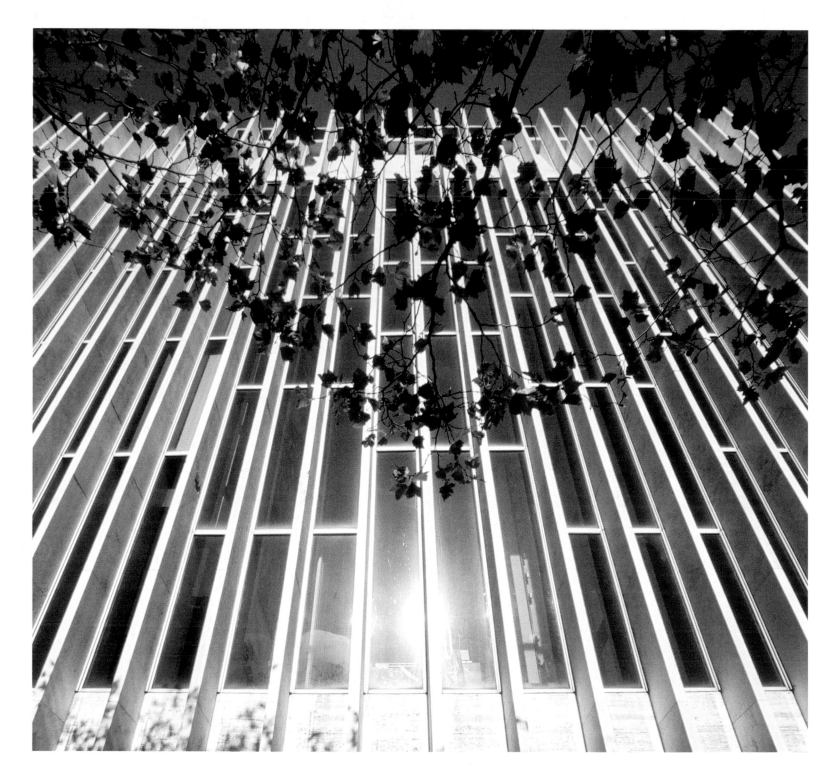

CONTENTS

INTRODUCTION

BELOW: Palace of the Governor, Santa Fe, New Mexico.

OPPOSITE: Mission of San Antonio (The Alamo), Texas.

This is a book about the buildings that North Americans live and work in, use in their daily lives, or visit occasionally to check out their cultural heritage and history. Because it is easy not to think too much about such things as houses, factories and offices, shopping centres, museums and bridges – and there are countless numbers of them, because they are needed for practical purposes – it is all too easy to lose sight of their artistic and cultural value and not to notice what a large part architects and architecture have played in the development of the North American way of life. One of the aims of this book, which describes in detail nearly 150 buildings and other structures from all over North America, is to show how their construction has

RIGHT: Lafitte's Blacksmith Shop, built before 1772 on Bourbon Street in the French Quarter of New Orleans.

BELOW: A Wild West town in Old Tucson, Arizona, with buildings of wooden construction.

both mirrored and influenced the evolution of a great society.

The architecture of North America has always been influenced, to a greater or lesser degree, by the architectural and cultural heritages of other nations, especially those of the continent's European forefathers. From the English, Spanish and French explorers and traders who crossed the Atlantic in ever-increasing numbers from the late 16th century, to the present day after the political upheavals of the 20th century made the United States and Canada havens for those fleeing persecution, Europeans have brought the building styles and techniques of

their native lands and cultures to their adopted countries.

When the first Europeans set foot on North America's eastern seaboard, there were no signs of permanent habitations built by the continent's indigenous peoples. For some of their first, makeshift shelters, therefore, the earliest settlers in New England copied the wigwams of the local Native American tribes. But when they began constructing more permanent structures, they built their dwellings, farms and meeting houses in styles as near as possible to the buildings they had left behind in England and The Netherlands, using the building tools and skills they had brought with them. Local building materials were scarce, however, though wood was available, but stone was in short supply; in fact, before brick kilns were built in the colonies, stone was often shipped from Europe, especially by the rich

Dutch merchants who had founded colonies in New Netherland. Otherwise, most buildings were made of wood.

It was not until the Spanish reached the south-western corner of the continent early in the 17th century that an indigenous building culture, that of the Pueblo Indians, was discovered. The oldest European-built structure still standing in North America, the Governor's Palace in Santa Fe (page), was built in adobe brick, with the clay for the bricks shaped Spanish-style in wooden boxes rather than by hand, as had been the practice of the Indians for centuries before. Doors and windows

BELOW LEFT: Paul Revere's House, Boston, Massachusetts.

LEFT. An example of a Barnstable cedar-shingle house, Cape Cod, Massachusetts.

followed the Pueblo Indian style and there was a typical Indian-style flat roof with projecting rafters. In the South-West today, this hybrid Spanish/Indian style, the only architectural style in North America to retain a strong indigenous influence, remains very much a force in local building design.

As far as the rest of the continent was concerned, the major influence on architectural styles in North America for nearly three centuries was European. In the newly independent United

OPPOSITE: Massachusetts Hall, Old Yard, Harvard University, Cambridge, Massachusetts (1720).

LEFT: Hollis Hall, Old Yard, Harvard University (1763). This was used to house George Washington's troops during the American Revolution.

The State Capitol, Hartford,
Connecticut – an example of
Renaissance-style architecture in
America designed by Richard M.
Upjohn (1828–1903).

States of America, when the Georgian-style architecture of 18th-century Britain was rejected by the leaders of the new republic, they turned to the Classical (and republican) architecture of Greece and Rome for inspiration, and Classicism was to influence the design of American public buildings until the mid 20th century: the first building of Washington's National Gallery of Art (page 123) was completed, in the Classical style, in 1941, only months before national outrage at the attack on Pearl Harbor precipitated America into the Second World War.

While design and decoration styles – Greek Revival, Romanesque and Renaissance, Beaux-Arts and Arts and Crafts – remained Europe-derived right up until the First World War, the construction of buildings was a different matter. In the last decades of the 19th century, the needs of the rapidly-growing and increasingly competitive and prosperous American economy led architects and engineers to adopt such European inventions as steel girders, plate glass and reinforced concrete and mould them to their own needs. As a result, the Chicago School's steel-

Frank Lloyd Wright's Taliesin West, Phoenix, Arizona, started in 1937.

framed, high-rise buildings, themselves made possible by such seemingly small-scale inventions as Elisha Otis's elevator, were to astonish the rest of the world.

As the 20th century progressed, American architecture, led in new directions by such architectural giants as the German-born Ludwig Mies van der Rohe and the American-born Frank Lloyd Wright, became that of the modern world. For a time, Modernism reigned supreme in architectural practices everywhere until, like all styles, it proved to be less perfectly suited to modern life than had first been envisaged and went out of fashion.

Much of the colour and vibrancy of American Postmodernism grew out of the culture of America itself, from fast-food diners to Disney cartoons by way of abstract-expressionist art. At the same time, the influence of architects and designers from cultures very different from that of America and Canada increased. In recent times, architects born in Europe, the Middle East, and China and Japan have been responsible for some of North America's most outstanding architecture. This will also apply to New York's devastated World Trade Center site (see page 430), whose new buildings will be designed, among others, by two Englishmen, a Japanese and a Polish-born American.

The main purpose of this book is to make North American architecture interesting to the general reader, to describe its variety of styles and designs and the many materials used in its creation, in language free of technicalities and the jargon-laden theory present in much of the recent writing on architecture. It offers a panoramic account of North American architecture,

from the late 16th century to the present. The buildings are included in the order in which they were built or, if the process took several years, in order of the year in which construction began. This cannot be a completely accurate way of placing the buildings in chronological order, for many of them spend years, even decades, as mere ideas in the architect's head or drawing board before the first shovelful of earth could be turned on site.

It is hoped the reader will see North American architecture in a new light and understand it for what it truly is – an expression of the culture and history of a great continent.

OPPOSITE: Crown Hall, Illinois Institute of Technology, Chicago (1950–56), by Ludwig Mies van der Rohe (see page 344).

FAR LEFT: Philip Johnson's 1976 Reflection Chapel on Thanksgiving Square, Dallas, Texas.

BELOW LEFT: The Montreal Biosphere, Quebec, Canada, a geodesic dome designed for the American Pavilion of Expo '67 by Richard Buckminster Fuller.

CHAPTER ONE

EARLY ARCHITECTURE
c.1600–c.1770

EARLY ARCHITECTURE
c.1600–c.1770

Castillo de San Marcos, St. Augustine, Florida, built 1672–1756. (See page 43 et seq.)

The earliest European settlement of North America was that of St. Augustine, founded by the Spanish in the area they called Florida in 1565. St. Augustine, with its great fort, the Castillo de San Marcos, built a century later, looked to medieval European fortifications for its inspiration. Later, exploring north from Mexico, the Spanish came to what is now New Mexico and Arizona, where they found the uniquely styled adobe houses of the Pueblo Indians, who had been using these forms and materials since the seventh century AD. The Spanish were quick to absorb these indigenous influences in, for example, Santa Fe, founded in 1609. This they built in a style that brilliantly syncretized both Pueblo Indian and Spanish architectural forms that remain influential in the south-western states to this day.

When other Europeans began to arrive in North America in the early 17th century – English and Dutch traders and settlers along the eastern seaboard and the French in Canada – they could have been forgiven for thinking no permanent habitations existed in this vast land, there being nothing to suggest otherwise. Therefore, with little to inspire them, and with few raw materials other than trees at their disposal, they kept to what they knew, building their first real houses, and indeed, all their buildings for the next three centuries or so, in adaptations of styles they had been familiar with in Europe.

The kitchen of the Governor's Palace, San Antonio, Texas, is an example of an early adobe building (see also pages 75 and 76).

But in the meantime, the first English settlers of what were to be the first 13 colonial states, made do with primitive shelters that were makeshift, crude and could be quickly built; these included dugouts, wattle-and-daub cabins, tents and wigwams, often made of sailcloth taken from the ships that had recently transported them across the Atlantic. With such skimpy structures to protect them from the harsh winter, it is not surprising that, of the company that stepped ashore from the *Mayflower* in Plymouth in December 1620, half were dead before spring arrived.

25

OPPOSITE: The Whipple House, Ipswich, Massachusetts. The original house was possibly constructed as early as 1638 by John Fawn and was later sold to John Whipple (the Elder). It was enlarged over the years, with a substantial addition in 1670.

LEFT: A Connecticut 'gingerbread' clapboard house in East Haddam.

RIGHT: The colonial splendour of Drayton Hall, a former plantation house in Charleston, South Carolina. It has been dated to between 1738 and 1742, but the architect is unknown.

BELOW: Fort Crailo, Rensselaer, New York, built c.1642 (see page 38).

OPPOSITE: A grand mansion in Charleston, South Carolina.

But the settlers that survived had brought their building skills and tools with them and quickly began to construct more permanent shelters. Hewn planks, squared timbers and flat boards were soon being incorporated into houses that had doors, windows and chimneys rising up through sod-covered roofs. Within a year or two, the typical timber-framed, clapboard-clad, shingle-roofed house of the New England states and Middle Colonies was being built in increasing numbers.

With a cellar below ground level and one-and-a-half or two storeys above, these houses, single-roomed at first, expanded as families and fortunes grew. Floor plans were extended to two, three or four rooms, wings were added at the sides and lean-tos

at the back, the latter creating what was often referred to as the 'saltbox' shape. They would have been quite familiar to friends and relatives back home, most of them living in the south-eastern counties of England.

The Puritan settlers in New England constructed larger buildings alongside their houses to serve as meeting houses and churches, creating an architectural form perfectly suited to their simple, austere religious needs. In England, the Puritans had been accustomed to meeting in houses or halls, taverns or even barns, often quietly hidden away in the countryside. Such places had no altars, choir stalls, naves or transepts. They were much more likely to be squarish in shape rather than extended oblongs divided by a central aisle. When the first Puritans arrived in New England, then, it was not surprising that they should build their first meeting places in a similarly unpretentious style.

Traders from the lowlands of Holland and Flanders also arrived in North America early in the 17th century, colonizing an area covering the Hudson river valley, the west half of Long Island, and the northern part of New Jersey, while fur traders, exploring up the valley of the Hudson river set up a stockaded trading post near present-day Albany in 1614.

For nearly half a century, these people developed and governed the region, naming it New Netherland, with New Amsterdam its largest town. For several generations the region was dominated by great estates: two patroonships were established by the Dutch and nine extensive manors were erected by the English after 1671. Of them all, the largest and most successful was the huge Dutch patroonship of Rensselaerswyck and the English manor of the same name that followed it in 1685.

Williamsburg, the colonial capital of Virginia from 1699, was built to a gridiron plan of major and minor axes that were inspired by European cities built during the Renaissance.

The transformation of the settlement of Middle Plantation into the planned town of Williamsburg, complete with a college, a capitol and a governor's palace, all in coolly Classical style, came at a time when the building styles of the early colonial period were giving way to what would be called 'Georgian'. By this time the colonies of the eastern seaboard were flourishing and becoming increasingly wealthy, and men of substance and distinction automatically turned to England and its aristocratic classes for cultural, social, and architectural inspiration. In truth, the transformation of American architecture from 'Colonial' to 'Georgian' was in the making well before the Hanoverian George I ascended the throne in Britain in 1714.

ABOVE: This historic terrace in Walnut Street, Philadelphia, Pennsylvania, includes Bishop White House (1787).

RIGHT: The nearby Todd House was built in 1775.

By the end of the 17th century, the people of the eastern seaboard states had established towns and cities which they considered the equal of anything in Europe – largely, it must be admitted, because they had been assiduously copied from European models. Many places did not evolve naturally but were planned – Charleston in 1680, Philadelphia in 1682, Annapolis in 1694 and Williamsburg in 1699 being typical examples.

Architectural historians point to a late-1680s example in Boston – the Foster-Hutchinson House – as the first truly Georgian house in America. When William Penn visited Philadelphia in 1700, he found a thriving city full of tall brick houses in the English style. He stayed in an elegant three-storeyed brick house, called the Slate House because of its slate roof (hipped, not steeply gabled and with Georgian dormers), that had been designed in a clearly Classical style by an English architect.

England's Surveyor-General, Sir Christopher Wren, who

First mention of the John Greenhow Boot and Shoe Store, in Williamsburg, Virginia, was made in 1766.

provided many plans for important buildings in Britain's American colonies and was the inspiration behind many more, was, like European architects of the age, strongly influenced by the buildings of the Renaissance, when the architecture of Classical Greece and Rome was rediscovered in Europe. The tenets and rules of Renaissance architecture underlay the Georgian architecture of 18th-century Britain and America, and it was not until the American colonies began to chaff at the restraining bit of British rule later in the 18th century that the Georgian style was consciously rejected in favour of one that reflected more truly that of the Classical, republican world.

OPPOSITE: Bruton Church, Williamsburg, Virginia, built in the 1770s.

BELOW LEFT: Christiana Campbell's Tavern, Williamsburg, Virginia, built in 1774.

BELOW: The Governor's Palace, Santa
Fe, New Mexico.

OPPOSITE & PAGE 36: The Adam
Thoroughgood House, near Norfolk,
Virginia.

Governor's Palace
Santa Fe, New Mexico
1610–14

Santa Fe's Governor's Palace is the oldest European-built
structure in North America and the oldest public building in the
United States. It was built as a residence for New Mexico's first
governor, Don Pedro de Peralta, who established the capital of
this new Spanish province at Santa Fe in 1609.

Today, the Governor's Palace fills one whole side of Santa

Fe's central plaza. When it was first built, it was just one
building, though the most important one, in a fortified
presidio, a vast walled enclosure which also contained barracks
and a powder magazine for the Spanish troops, along with
offices, stores and prisons. There is nothing to distinguish the
Governor's Palace from the buildings that surround it, but
neither is the palace dominated by them. Santa Fe maintains a
tight control on building in the city. No building is very high
and all – houses, churches, government buildings – tend to
follow Native American models, in that they are built of
adobe brick, have the distinctive Indian windows and door
moulded into curves, and the typical flat roofs with projecting
rafters (vigas), many made from a local tree, the palo verde
(*Parkinsonia floridum*).

The Governor's Palace is a long, low building with a flat,
sod-covered roof with projecting vigas. Running the length of its
front is a covered loggia or portal supported on wooden posts.
Native Americans built the palace and it was constructed very
much in Pueblo Indian style; the roof is typically so, though the
adobe clay that has been used for centuries is not simply piled
up and moulded into shape in the ancient Pueblo way. Instead,
the builders followed a method, introduced by the Spanish,
which involved precasting the clay in wooden boxes to make
large bricks and then sun-drying them. Other signs that the
Spanish were involved in the building of the palace are its
portal, with its bracket capitals, the central enclosed patio, and
the wooden frames that surround doors and windows.

Twenty-eight Spanish governors of New Mexico lived in the
palace after 1692. From 1848, when the United States took

control of New Mexico from the Mexicans, until 1909, the palace was occupied by the American governors of the territory. It was carefully restored in 1909 and today the Palace of the Governors of New Mexico houses one of the four Santa Fe museums that make up the Museum of New Mexico. Its Native American connection is still maintained, and Indians from a nearby reservation set out rugs, jewellery and basketwork for sale to visitors in the shelter of the loggia.

Adam Thoroughgood House
nr. Norfolk, Virginia
c.1636–40

This simple but solidly built brick-walled structure is the oldest house in Virginia. It is also, perhaps, the oldest in the English-speaking colonies, though the exact year of its building is not known.

The man who built it, Adam Thoroughgood, came to Virginia from England in 1621. Clearly an ambitious, get-up-and-go sort of person, Thoroughgood had by the end of the decade worked off his bond, having come to America as an indentured servant, and had gained enough standing in the colony to have been granted the status of a burgess. In 1636, he bought a piece of land on Lynnhaven Bay, where between this date and his death in 1640, he built a simple brick-walled house. The house was willed to his widow, Sarah, if indeed this was their house, and not another, much of the same period, that was built for or by one of Adam's sons.

The style of Adam Thoroughgood's house, and its internal plan, owes much to his English origins. Typical of smaller

Virginia farmhouses of the time, it is a low-eaved, steep-gabled, storey-and-a-half structure. The house in its original form had no dormer windows in the roof; these came later. The two small upstairs rooms under the steeply sloping roof were lit by small windows in the end walls. At ground level, the sliding-sash

windows were topped by low segmental arches and framed with glazed header bricks.

Adam and Sarah Thoroughgood entered their house through a front door, which was placed slightly off-centre, reflecting the fact that it led into the hall, the larger of the house's two ground-level rooms. The door was made of two layers of boards, set vertically on the outside and horizontally on the inside, and with the two layers held together by wrought-iron nails. Inside, the house had the simple two-roomed hall-and-parlour layout of many Virginia farmhouses of the period. There was a fireplace on the end walls of each room and a steep staircase, probably partitioned off from the room by a wainscot, going up from the hall to the upper floor.

The outlet for the large parlour fireplace, which was used both to heat the house and for cooking, was an imposing brick chimney projecting from the outside wall, while the chimney at the other end of the house was set within the wall. This chimney layout, typical of early buildings in Virginia, was quite distinct from early New England houses, which had central chimneys accommodating back-to-back fireplaces – another feature common to houses in England.

Fairbanks House
Dedham, Massachusetts
c.1637

This rambling, many-roofed house, is thought to be the oldest wood-framed house in America. It was originally built to the typical New England two-room plan, with a parlour and hall on either side of a large central chimney and with a small inner entrance porch, from which a staircase rose to the floor above, between the two rooms. Over the years it was added to, so that today the Fairbanks House is one of the best examples in America of the 'growing house' of colonial days.

The house was built by Jonathan Fayerbanke, a Yorkshireman who arrived in Boston in 1633, just four years after the city had been founded. In 1636 he moved on to the even newer settlement of Dedham, where he was allocated a house 'lott' of 12 acres (5 hectares), plus four acres of 'swampe' land. Within a year, a sturdy house, built around a frame of oak posts, was standing on his lot, its front facing south.

Fayerbanke's house was an 'upright' structure, with no overhanging eave and with the rafters joined together at the roof ridge (there was no ridge pole), while the walls, filled with clay daubed onto oak laths, were protected by clapboards. Inside, were the two rooms, a hall, and a rather smaller parlour with the small porch between, that were so typical of early New England houses. There is still some very old wide-boarded wainscoting in the hall that may have been installed at the time the house was built.

At the heart of the house was a very large brick chimney, with a fireplace to serve each of the house's two main rooms set back to back within it. This central chimney placing, a distinctive feature of medieval houses and inns in England, was also typical of houses in the New England colonies.

Jonathan Fayerbanke's land holdings increased considerably in the 20 years after he built his house, and as his standing in the community grew, so did his house. Early on, he lengthened his parlour and the chamber above it, in the form of a small hipped-roof section to the east of the main house, and there was soon a lean-to, with two extra rooms, added to the back.

In 1641 came a whole new east wing, with two rooms at ground level and one large one above, possibily built for Jonathan's son and his new bride: an American founding family was being established. Some time in the mid-1650s, another wing, with its own internal staircase, was added to the west of the house. This was entered through a door from the hall and may have been built to house Fayerbanke's hired men, who must have increased in number as the estate grew.

Fort Crailo
Rensselaer, New York
c.1642

Of the many manor houses that sprang up over the vast Dutch patroonship of Rensselaerswyck in the first half of the 17th century, only three remain. The most impressive of these is Fort Crailo at Rensselaer, on the Hudson, south of Albany.

This building was the administrative centre of the eastern side of the patroonship of Rensselaerswyck. It is not surprising, therefore, that the patroonship's founder, Kiliaen Van Rensselaer, sitting at his desk back in Amsterdam, was as concerned in detail with the building of Fort Crailo as he was with every other aspect of his North American domain (which he never saw). It is on record that in 1642 Van Rensselaer sent a ship from Holland, loaded with stone, bricks and tiles to New Netherland. That this building material was probably intended for use in the building of Fort Crailo is borne out by a stone inscribed 'K.V.R. 1642 ANNO DOMINI' set in a cellar wall at the fort. It is possible, of course, that the present house was built later than 1642, using materials rescued from an earlier building: after all, European brick and stone were rare in America and would not have been wasted. But Fort Crailo is solidly built and has loopholes in the ground-floor wall, indicating that it was built to serve as a fortress.

The bricks of Fort Crailo's outer walls are laid in the style known as Dutch cross bond. At roof-level, under the steep straight-lined gables, the bricks are laid in courses set at right angles to the gable edge, but join the horizontal bricks of the wall in a saw-tooth line. This arrangement, called a 'mouse-tooth' finish, helped to make exposed copings more weatherproof. It was a style of bricklaying well known in the Low Countries, and had even been taken by Flemings and Dutch into England's eastern counties, notably Norfolk, where such brick gables are referred to as 'tumbled in'.

Major additions were made to Fort Crailo in 1740, but the exterior remains a fine example of 17th-century Dutch New Netherland building style. The house came into the ownership of the state early in the 20th century and modern restoration has been carried out in the old style. Thus, on the exterior, the mullioned windows have diamond-paned casements, and also batten-type shutters, carried on wrought iron hinges. The roof is pantiled. Inside, wood is used extensively – for the heavy floor planks, the wainscoted wall panelling, made of vertical pine boards, and for much of the furniture.

Church of San Esteban, Acoma, New Mexico
c.1642

Acoma, an ancient pueblo in central New Mexico, sits atop an isolated mesa reaching nearly 370ft (113m) into the sky – hence its name 'Sky City'. To this centuries-old Native American village came the Franciscan Padre Juan Ramirez in 1629, intent on founding a mission. There was already a steep trail up to the

Church of San Esteban, Acoma, New Mexico.

village, but Ramirez built another, longer one, El Camino del Padre, to make sure his mission would get built. His reward was one of the most impressive of all the Spanish missions in New Mexico.

The great church of San Esteban del Rey at Acoma took more than 12 years to build, so difficult was the task. Everything, from the 40-ft (12-m) roof vigas, made of pine from the San Mateo mountains 30 miles (48km) away, to the soil for a burial ground and the padre's garden in the patio, had to be hauled up the steep trails to the top of the mesa on the backs of local labourers.

The church is a plain, thick-walled adobe building, facing east. Its facade is a bare wall, broken only by the entrance door and a window to light the choir loft over the front entrance. The ends of the roof vigas project from the walls in a random pattern, throwing shifting shadows on the walls where the sunlight catches them. Square towers flanking the side walls project boldly from the building and rise to belfries, revealing bells through typically rectilinear openings.

The large, cool and dimly-lit interior is basically a long rectangle, narrowing at the western end to a polygonal sanctuary. It has an earthen-floored nave and whitewashed walls. The roof is splendid, its vigas adorned with strongly carved and painted corbels. A great painting, executed in vigorous Pueblo Indian style, fills the end wall of the sanctuary.

Father Ramirez, or perhaps a later friar (because of its size, San Esteban was usually inhabited by two friars) built a covered walk over his patio. This unusual luxury in the New Mexico missions accounts, perhaps, for the attractiveness of the padre's garden, described so finely in Willa Cather's *Death Comes for the Archbishop*. It helps to make a visit to the Mission of San Esteban del Rey at Acoma particularly memorable.

Pieter Claesen Wyckoff House
Flatlands, Brooklyn, New York City
c.1652

In the 17th century, settlers from the Low Countries built five towns at the western end of Long Island, in southern New Netherland. The settlers were a mixture of Dutch, Flemish, Walloon and French Huguenots and most of them were farmers. The farmhouse built by Peter Wyckoff near the town of Nicuw Amersfoort (Flatlands), which itself eventually merged with the town of Breuckelen (Brooklyn), was one of the earliest constructed by these hard-working people, and it has been one of the longest lasting.

Most of the houses built in or near these five towns were of frame construction, Long Island being well wooded but short of stone. Pieter Wyckoff's house was no exception: it had very long roof shingles, a size and shape favoured by Flemish and Walloon settlers, that were hand-hewn from cedar wood. The house had the typical Dutch panelled doors and window shutters, and two chimneys, one at each end of the house – also a Dutch characteristic.

While the date cannot be confirmed, there is no doubt that the house was extended more than once; in fact, close study of the floor and roof beams indicate clearly that the house was extended by nearly a half some time after it was built. Much later, perhaps in the 1780s, a whole new wing was added.

Originally, it probably had the steep roof found on many early Dutch-built houses. Later, probably when the house was extended, the roof acquired gables and a lower pitch, with curved projecting eaves at the front and back. For many years, American architects considered such eaves a truly American architectural innovation, but later historians, researching old building styles in Flanders, found the eaves, like roof shingles, to be a Flemish tradition.

Castillo de San Marcos
St. Augustine, Florida
1672–1756

The Castillo de San Marcos is the oldest masonry-built stronghold in the United States, the star-shaped fortress having replaced a succession of wooden forts that had stood on the site since 1565. It was built by the Spanish to guard their possessions in Florida from the increasing encroachment of

OPPOSITE, BELOW & PAGE 44: Castillo de San Marcos, St. Augustine, Florida.

other European nations, especially the British up in Georgia, and from pirates.

The major part of the Castillo de San Marco was built between 1672 and 1675, by which time three walls had been completed and a wooden palisade enclosed the fourth side. It was not until 1756 that the fort assumed its final shape, with the bastions, moat and outworks that visitors see today in their finished form. Its first stage cost so much that the king of Spain asked if its curtains and bastions had been constructed of solid silver. He would perhaps have complained less bitterly if he could have foreseen that this massive fort, its walls 14ft (4.3m) thick, would never be taken in battle. In 1740, General James Oglethorpe, making the third and last unsuccessful British attempt on the fort in the 18th century, found that his cannonballs made hardly a dent in the walls and dubbed it 'the sponge fort'.

Far from being strengthened with silver, the sloping walls were made of massive blocks of coquina limestone, quarried on nearby Anastasia Island and cemented with oyster-lime mortar. But it was not only the thickness and strength of the walls that made the fort so impenetrable. It was also outstandingly well designed, its Spanish military engineer-designer, Ignacio Diaz, having made good use of the best features of European fortresses designed after the invention of gunpowder in the Middle Ages.

From its single, heavily-guarded entrance, complete with drawbridge, to the diamond-shaped bastions set at each corner to maximize firepower and make attackers vulnerable to crossfire, the fort was virtually impregnable. Its powder magazines were buried deep, so that even if mortars had managed to penetrate the 35-ft (11-m) ramparts, they would still not have reached the fort's

ammunition stores. Diaz also surrounded his fort with a moat, connected to the bay along which St. Augustine was built, so that water levels in it rose and fell with the tide.

After Florida became permanently part of the United States, the Castillo de San Marcos was used more often as a prison than a fort. Among its inmates were prisoners from the Seminole wars and, in 1886, Geronimo's three wives, a dozen chiefs and 500 Apache warriors. Today, the fort, one of the most impressive pieces of Spanish architecture in the United States, is a national monument.

Paul Revere House
Boston, Massachusetts
c.1676

Although this house had already had a lengthy existence of its own before Paul Revere, the great American patriot, came to live in it during the last 30 years of the 18th century, the fact that it now bears his name seems entirely justified and has possibly ensured its survival.

This is Boston's last surviving 17th-century house. It was built after the great fire that devastated the town in 1676, on a narrow, crooked plot of land in North Square, then close to the docks and an area of town dominated by the trades connected with shipping.

The house that John Jeffs originally built on the site probably had only one room – suggested by the presence in the front hall of a deeply recessed fireplace with a bake oven. Quite early in the house's life, a kitchen was added in a crooked L-shape at the back, a line dictated by the shape of the building lot. Above the

RIGHT & OPPOSITE: The Paul Revere
House, Boston, Massachusetts.

kitchen's back door, the roof had a prominent overhang.

By the time Paul Revere quietly left the house by way of the back door on 18 April 1775, to ride to Lexington with the warning of a British attack, his house had long been a substantial three-storey building; it needed to be large, since Revere, a silversmith and freemason, was also father to 16 children.

By the end of the 19th century, by which time better-off Bostonians had moved away from the area around the docks, the house was a tenement and in a poor state of repair. It was not pulled down, almost certainly because Paul Revere had lived there, but became the subject of a special survey and inspection in 1908, when it was restored to its late-17th-century form.

Today, the house has an impressive facade, with an overhang and parallel rather than feather-edged clapboards. The diamond-leaded windows with wooden shutters, the heavy wooden front door and the roof shingles are all as they would have been in the 17th century. Inside, the hall is typically of its time, but the second-storey room is plastered, panelled and painted in the style of a century later.

Senate House
Kingston, New York
c.1676–95

In their towns and villages in the lower reaches of the Hudson valley, the Dutch built many houses of stone, rather than their preferred brick, because stone was more readily to hand. Nowadays, of course, an 'old stone house' – spoken almost as one word in reverential tones – is a very desirable property to own.

The pleasant town of Kingston, the largest in the Catskills,

was founded in 1653 by the Dutch, who named it Wiltwyck. The town's Stockade District still has many well-preserved stone houses dating to the early days of Dutch settlement, one of the most interesting of which, today called the Senate House, was built by Wessel Wesselse ten Broek between 1676 and 1695.

Ten Broek used rough-faced stones, all cut to much the same size, for the walls of his house. He carried the stonework up to the tip of the end gable, above the garret windows, rather than using shingles to face this section of wall, as was more common. Like many Dutch houses of the period, ten Broek's house was only one room deep. Its three rooms were built in a line, with the two end rooms each having an outside door. The gable roof had a lower pitch than the steep-roofed houses built by the Dutch further up the Hudson river.

Wessel Wesselse ten Broek's house acquired its present name, the Senate House, after the first New York State Senate met there in 1777. This was the year the British drove the provincial congress from New York City and Kingston briefly became the state's first capital. British troops then came along and set fire to the building, burning the interior woodwork and the roof. When the roof was rebuilt, its shallow sloping dormers were constructed in the early Dutch style. Today the Senate House is a State Historic Site.

The Old Ship Meeting House
Hingham, Massachusetts
1681

The oldest surviving church in the English colonies in America is the Puritan Old Ship Meeting House at Hingham in

Massachusetts. Built in 1681, it is a particularly fine example of the frame-and-post, clapboard, shingle-roofed Puritan meeting houses of New England. Its name derives both from the traditional belief that it was built by ship's carpenters and from the fact that inside, because its splendid roof-framing was left exposed, it resembled an inverted ship's hull.

Since the members of the congregation in Hingham were to be directly taxed to pay for the meeting house, they had a big say in its construction. Its squarish size – 45 x 55ft (14 x 17m) – and the height of its frame posts (20ft /6m) were determined in a vote by the town. These dimensions made the meeting hall large and lofty indeed, and also ensured the structure's belfry soared high above the community. The belfry, surrounded by a small railed platform, was set centrally on the roof. This meant that the bell rope hung down in the centre of the meeting room, swinging in the midst of the congregation.

Inside, there was no internal ceiling, and the trusses and side struts of the roof-framing were clearly visible. Nor was there any sign of an altar, which would have been the main feature of the traditional long-aisled English church. The pulpit was the main focus of the Puritan meeting house, and so the congregation's benches were set lengthways, facing the pulpit which stood in the middle of one of the long walls. The main entrance door was set in the centre of the opposite long wall, behind the benches.

Half a century after it was built, the Old Ship Meeting House was enlarged. Later in the 18th century, the rigidly uncomfortable oak benches were replaced by pews, a gallery was added on three sides, the windows became sliding-sashed and wood-framed and two porches in Georgian style were added. After a vote by the

The Parson Capen House, Topsfield, Massachusetts.

congregation, a flat ceiling was put in under the tie beams, so that the roof-framing was hidden. When the meeting house underwent a restoration in the 1930s, the ceiling was removed and the roof framing was once again revealed, in all its ship-like magnificence.

Parson Capen House
Topsfield, Massachusetts
1683

The parsonage built for the Reverend Joseph Capen at Topsfield has become a place of pilgrimage for anyone interested in the architecture of colonial America. Thanks largely to the efforts of the Topsfield Historical Society, which acquired the house in 1913, it has come to be seen by many architectural historians as the most perfect of all the remaining New England colonial period houses.

Even today it looks as if it had been recently transported from 17th-century England, brought from some farm in the rolling countryside near the Essex hamlet of Toppesfield to be re-erected on a wooded hillside in Massachusetts.

Outside, the Parson Capen house has a dignified simplicity. It is a clapboard house, with a shingle roof with strong overhangs at the front and gable ends. Inside, the house has the two-room plan typical of many New England colonial houses. It has two main rooms – parlour and hall – separated by a small porch from which a staircase, built in front of the centrally-placed chimney, rises steeply to the rooms above.

Perhaps because the house was built for a Puritan minister, its parlour was larger than usual, larger than the hall, in fact. Its size meant that the builders had to put in two large summer beams, rather than the more usual one, to support the weight of the floor above. Both parlour and hall were given very wide fireplaces, with the one in the hall – often referred to as the 'kitchen' in early documents having an oak mantel beam 16-in (41-cm) square.

The house has been furnished with scrupulous attention to 17th-century detail. There is much wood, including wide sanded floorboards, wainscoted walls and splendidly solid roof beams, as well as many fine pieces of wooden furniture and utensils. The house is simple, frugal without seeming poverty-stricken, and with an innate dignity of its own. It is easy to believe the Reverend Joseph Capen was much the same sort of man.

John Ward House
Salem, Massachusetts
1684

Salem, where the colony of Massachusetts was first founded, is known for its many gabled buildings, so it is no coincidence that it is the place where the town's most famous son, Nathaniel Hawthorne, set one of his best-known novels, *The House of the Seven Gables* (1851). Here also can be found the impressively gabled John Ward House.

Today a museum of colonial life in the grounds of the Essex Institute, the John Ward House began life as quite a small dwelling of only one room, a parlour, with a single room above. It also had from its beginnings the large chimney and the small porch with staircase opposite the front door typical of New England colonial houses. It was unusual at the time in that it had an overhang at the front and the end, giving the upper chamber on the second floor extra space.

Some time later, perhaps because of his growing family, John Ward extended his house, adding a summer-beamed hall with a very large fireplace to the east of the chimney, which was now within the house rather than on an end wall. He also extended the overhang on the front of the house, but did not carry it on around the east-end wall.

Some time before he died, John Ward added a lean-to across the entire back of his house, so long that it could be divided into three rooms. The roof of this lean-to broke the pitch of the house's original roof.

The facade of the house has many asymmetrical features, suggesting that its builder, like many in the early days of colonial America, had a fairly relaxed attitude to architectural regularity. The front door is off-centre, as is the chimney behind it inside the house, reflecting the fact that the hall is narrower than the parlour. The central window on the second floor is set noticeably to one side of the front door below it, and the two front gables

OPPOSITE: Sir Christopher Wren's
College of William and Mary,
Williamsburg, Virginia.

have different widths and roof pitches. These all indicate that the colonial house was intended to grow with its owner's changing needs: pulling down and starting again was regarded as a waste of time, and materials in a young colony were in short supply.

Friends Meeting House
Flushing, Queens, New York, NY
1694

The Puritan community that built this simple yet sturdy wooden meeting house, probably never imagined it would still be standing more than three centuries later, and that it would still be in use as a place of religious worship.

Nor could they have imagined that the quiet open country in which it stood would have completely disappeared under the inexorable expansion of the city of New York, or that it would end up only yards from a noisy, polluted ten-lane freeway, the Northern Boulevard. The Friends Meeting House in Queens has not had an uninterrupted life as a religious building, however. From 1776 to 1783 it was occupied by the British, who turned it into a jail, a hayloft and a field hospital.

But once one enters the building, all this ceases to matter. The British tenure, in terms of the age of the building, was brief and no sign remains of the other uses to which it was subjected. Today, the building retains the familiar meeting-house layout: pews set across the length of the building, facing the pulpit, bell rope hanging down from the centre of the roof, plain whitewashed walls. There is, too, the familiar air of quiet austerity and strong religious faith. It is truly an oasis of simple calm in a busy metropolis.

College of William and Mary
Williamsburg, Virginia
1695–1702

It is almost certain that Sir Christopher Wren, architect of St. Paul's Cathedral in London and of other magnificent buildings in England, was the inspiration and possibly even the man who drew up the original plans behind this first college to be built in Virginia. It was named in honour of King William III, who had granted a royal charter for its building in 1693, and his wife, Queen Mary, both sovereigns in their own right.

It is believed, too, that the men building the college – before work was even started on the capitol or a house for the governor – had before them as they worked plans drawn up by Wren, then England's Surveyor-General, and brought to Virginia by the Reverend James Blair, along with a master builder called Thomas Hadley and £2,000 to fund the job.

The plan from England was for a U-shaped structure, the main building having an open, brick-paved piazza behind. The building was flanked by low wings, one to house the college dining hall (or refectory), the other the chapel. The cornerstone was laid in 1695 and two sides of a planned quadrangle of buildings, similar to a typical Oxford College, were completed by 1702. This building burned down in 1705 and was rebuilt, the chapel wing being completed in 1732.

A visitor, commenting on 'The College' in 1722, described it as 'beautiful and commodious, being first modelled by Sir Christopher Wren… and is not altogether unlike Chelsea Hospital…'. And indeed, many signs of the great architect's work were to be seen in this building, which departed so completely from the old medieval English Gothic traditions used in so many early buildings in America, that it is now seen as the earliest example of mature Renaissance style in the colonies.

The college had the same formal symmetry as Wren's Chelsea Hospital and his additions at Hampton Court Palace. Built of brick, it was four-storeyed (counting the attic and the English-style basement as two floors). It had a round-arched portal, with balcony and gable, in the centre of the front facade, and a lofty cupola placed in the middle of the roof line to accentuate the central axis. The sash windows, their divider bars heralding the full Georgian style to come later in the century, were set uniformly on either side of the portal. Also in anticipation of Georgian style, the dormers at attic level were narrow and had the same sash windows with divider bars as the lower floors. At roof level, Wren ignored any thought of a Palladian-style low classic balustrade, and included a sharply pitched gable in his roof in order to continue the building's vertical axis.

The building housed the college's teaching faculty, all the students, the Native American scholars and the president and his wife. In 1723, Brafferton Hall, named after Brafferton Manor in England, which supplied some of the Hall's income, was erected as a school for Native Americans. Some nine years later, a twin building, the President's House, was built facing Brafferton Hall, the two together making a formal approach to the college's main building.

Such was the College of William and Mary, where George Wythe, Thomas Jefferson, George Mason, James Monroe and other leaders of the American Revolution all learned about and argued over democracy and law. Thus the college contributed to

53

RIGHT & OPPOSITE: The Old Dutch Church, Sleepy Hollow, Tarrytown, New York.

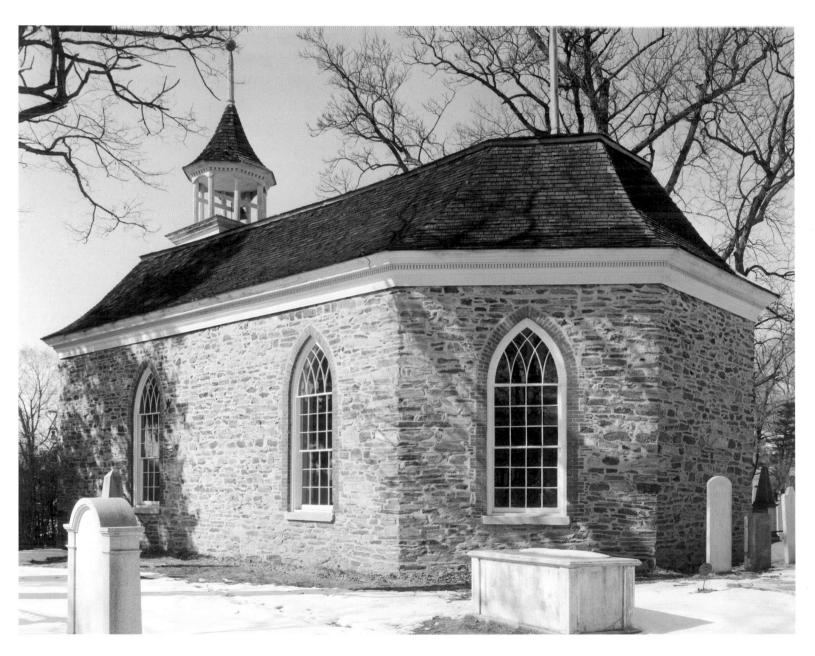

OPPOSITE & PAGE 58: Governor's
Palace, Williamsburg, Virginia.

Williamsburg's role as the birthplace of the revolutionary spirit
in America.

Old Dutch Church (Sleepy Hollow Church)
Tarrytown, New York
1697

Frederick Philipse, employed by the Dutch West Indies
Company, made a fortune in trade in New Amsterdam in the
second half of the 17th century. He built Sleepy Hollow Church
in Tarrytown on his own extensive land holdings, which included
nearby Philipsborough Manor (now Philipsburg Manor, an
attractive educational outdoor museum), in the lower Hudson
valley. The church actually dates from 1685, though the
congregation did not use it until 1697.

Unlike many of the Dutch-built churches in New
Netherland, which were based on the octagonal-planned
Protestant churches of Holland, Frederick Philipse's church was
almost rectangular in shape, and larger than was common in the
Dutch Hudson valley towns. This was as far as Philipse was
prepared to go in demonstrating his wealth. His church was
strictly Calvinist in both its inner and outer severity.

Its walls were of uniformly-shaped rubblestone, and the front
facade was broken only by an entrance door and pointed-arch
windows with simple rectangular-paned glazing. The interior was
as plain as other Dutch churches, with the seating arranged to
face the pulpit, which was set, raised on a pedestal, opposite the
entrance door.

Frederick Philipse came nearest to the distinctive octagonal
shape of the Dutch settlers' churches with the belfry of his
church. An open octagonal in shape, the belfry was set on a
typical Flemish gambrel-shaped roof, its bell having been cast in
Holland in 1685, when it was shipped to America. Frederick
Philipse left his mark on the church his generosity had made
possible, but in a characteristically modest way: he had his initials
cut into the wrought-iron weather vane which topped the belfry –
well out of reach and out of sight.

Next to the church is Sleepy Hollow Cemetery, once simply
the Tarrytown cemetery but renamed in 1996, along with the rest
of North Tarrytown. This was in honour of Washington Irving,
the town's most famous son, in order to 'keep that beautiful and
umbrageous neighborhood sacred from the anti-poetical and all-
leveling axe'. Irving is himself buried in the churchyard.

Governor's Palace
Williamsburg, Virginia
1706–20

In an opulent style justifying its name, the house created for the
royal governors of Virginia was the culmination of a building
programme that had been set in motion when the colonial capital
was moved from Jamestown to a small village known as the
Middle Plantation in the last quarter of the 17th century.
Renamed Williamsburg in honour of King William III, it was the
capital of Virginia from 1699 to 1779.

The Middle Plantation was not only renamed, it was also
replanned, being the fourth planned town in the American
colonies. A splendid city was laid out, its main axis being an
avenue named Duke of Gloucester Street, nearly a mile (1.6km)
long and 100ft (30m) wide. The College of William and Mary

and the Capitol were built facing each other at the avenue's western and eastern ends.

The northern arm of a minor axis, which cut across Duke of Gloucester Street about midway along, was called Palace Green and would have the Governor's Palace as its terminus. In 1706 the Assembly appropriated a lavish sum – £3,000 – for the palace, and chose Henry Cary, who had recently finished work on the Capitol, to supervise its building. Although no architect was named in any of the many documents covering the project, historians believe it was most probably designed in London, and that Sir Christopher Wren had a hand in the work.

Certainly, the Governor's Palace bears many of the hallmarks of a Wren building. There is the Classically symmetrical facade, with the narrow verticals of its ranges of windows, the steep roof, and the slender cupola set centrally on the roof, already seen before in the College of William and Mary. One very unusual feature – at least for a building in Virginia at this time – was a roof-deck balustrade which, with the pilastered chimneys at either end of the roofline, helped to lead the eye upward.

Building began in 1706 and by 1709 was far enough advanced for roof slate to be imported. The Assembly had to come up with more money for finishings and embellishments in 1710 and 1713, and the building was not formally declared complete until 1720, by which time it was the finest residence in the American colonies. For the next 60 years, the Governor's Palace, in its lovely setting of formal gardens and park, was not only the centre of public life in Williamsburg, but also the venue for balls, 'illuminations' and lavish entertainments.

When Thomas Jefferson moved the capital to Richmond

during the Revolutionary War, the palace was used as a hospital for casualties from the seige of Yorktown. It was destroyed by fire in December 1781. The beautiful, richly furnished building, set in formal gardens complete with a box maze, through which today's visitors are led by costumed guides, is a superb restoration, carefully carried out in fine detail. It is one of the architectural jewels of colonial Williamsburg.

Fort Chambly
nr. Montreal, Quebec, Canada
1709–11

Early French explorers and fur traders in North America left behind them, either in Canada, where Quebec was founded in 1608, or in Louisiana, founded in 1682, few buildings solid enough to be still standing centuries later. The one distinctively

Fort Chambly, near Montreal, Quebec, Canada.

French building that survives from the early colonial period in North America is Fort Chambly, near Montreal. Chambly was one of several forts built in the valley of the Richelieu river to defend Montreal, first from attacks by Iroquois, and then from British and American troops.

It was designed and built by the French regime's chief engineer in Canada, Josué Boisberthelot de Beaucourt. He replaced a wooden fort, built in 1665 by Jacques de Chambly, with a magnificent stone edifice, the plan for which was based on designs by Louis XIV's military architect and siege engineer, Sebastien Le Prestre de Vauban.

Fort Chambly is basically a square, with bastions at each corner.

Old State House
Boston, Massachusetts
1712–13; rebuilt 1748

Architecturally, the Old State House manages to hold its own, at least on the outside, though its internal layout was not well served by 19th-century restorers. Today, however, situated as it is on Boston's Freedom Trail, it is a model of 18th-century elegance in the midst of skyscrapers.

The Old State House was a seat of colonial government for Massachusetts and for the city of Boston for most of the 18th century, until it was replaced in 1798 by the Massachusetts State House, designed by Charles Bulfinch. George III was proclaimed king from the balcony of the Old State House in 1760, and the Declaration of Independence was also made from there on 18 July 1776. On the same day 200 years later,

George III's descendant, Elizabeth II, made a quite different, definitely non-revolutionary, appearance on the balcony during a state visit to the United States to mark the Bicentenary.

The Old State House replaced a 50-year-old wooden Town House that was burned down in October 1711 in a fire that destroyed many of Boston's oldest and most historic buildings. Old engravings show the 1712–13 building to have been a brick structure, in simple Wren-moving-towards-Georgian style. In 1747 this building was also destroyed by fire, along with most of the documents that recorded its design and building.

Within a year it had been rebuilt, this time in a fully-realized Georgian style. The main entrance was at street level at the west end of the building. An angular pediment was set above the door, and round windows adorned the gable end above. At the east end of the building was an even more splendid doorway, framed by Corinthian pilasters and topped by a pediment. A small balcony on this pediment at second-floor level could be reached from the Governor's Council Chamber.

Within, the ground floor was occupied almost entirely by a large hall, in which a row of ten Doric columns supported the second floor. This hall was used as a merchant's exchange. To judge by an early description of the building as 'a very Grand Brick Building, Arch'd all Round', it may well have been an open space on the ground floor, like an English market hall, for some years after it was built.

When the building became the State House of the new Commonwealth of Massachusetts in 1776, there was a considerable amount of internal rebuilding and replanning to

OPPOSITE & LEFT: Old State House, Boston, Massachusetts.

RIGHT: Old State House, Boston, Massachusetts.

OPPOSITE & PAGE 64: The Mission of San Antonio (The Alamo), Texas.

fit it for its new role. Once it had lost this role to the new Massachusetts State House in 1798, the building was used for numerous purposes, notably as the Boston City Hall in the 1830s, for which it was again replanned inside, this time in Greek Revival style.

The Old State House deteriorated badly in the 19th century and came close to being pulled down. But the Declaration of Independence had been read here and George Washington had been cheered to the echo during a triumphal visit to Boston in 1789. So, in 1881–82 it was restored, and the old British lion and unicorn were reinstated as they once were when they proudly presided over the deliberations of governors appointed by George II and George III.

Mission of San Antonio (The Alamo)
San Antonio, Texas
1718 (church built 1744–57)

Founded in 1718, as part of the settlement of San Antonio begun by Don Martín de Alarcón, Spanish Governor of the province of Texas, this was one of some dozen missions sited along remote stretches of the San Antonio river in the early years of the 18th century. Of those 12 missions, only five survive, all of them near San Antonio – the 'mission capital of Texas'.

Of the five, the mission of San Antonio de Valero is the most famous. Known today simply as 'the Alamo', it occupies an immortal place in American history. The Alamo was the scene of the last desperate fight of 189 Texan volunteers, including Colonel James Bowie and Davy Crockett, who held out for 13 days against

5,000 Mexican troops led by General Santa Anna, in the Texas War of Independence in 1836.

In the train of soldiers, settlers and 2,000 head of cattle, that Don Alarcón brought with him to San Antonio in 1691, was a Franciscan friar, Fray Antonio Olivares, who founded the mission in San Antonio. He called it San Antonio de Valero in honour of the Viceroy of New Spain, the Marquess of Valero, and St. Anthony of Padua.

The Alamo, set up primarily as a school for Native Americans, was of less architectural merit than other Texas missions. Within its large enclosure it sheltered shops, houses and storehouses besides the school. The mission church was not begun until 1744. Building was slow, perhaps because it had been designed in a grand, European style, and it was not completed until 1757. It was also, apparently, not well built, because its bell towers, the vault over the nave and the dome all collapsed five years later.

The church was not repaired and it was as a roofless shell filled with rubble that it sheltered Jim Bowie, Davy Crockett and the rest during the siege of 1836. By this time the old mission, renamed Pueblo del Alamo after the home town of the Spanish cavalry unit based there – Alamo de Parras, in Mexico – had been secularized for 35 years. Today, the restored Alamo, with a wooden roof added and the facade, with its arched top, rebuilt, is the biggest attraction in downtown San Antonio.

The chapel retains the elaborately carved stone portal, flanked by niches and two pairs of spirally fluted columns, that surrounded the entrance door of the old church. In the chapel there is a fine display of emotive battle memorabilia, including

The Alamo, detail of entrance.

letters sent home by soldiers preparing to die. The Long Barracks of the Pueblo del Alamo is now a museum, where visitors may see a video show outlining the mission's history and the course of the battle.

Within the Alamo's 4-acre (1.6-hectare) grounds, with their lush gardens, all is peace and tranquillity. It is easy to forget the noise and bustle of the busy town beyond the walls, but not easy to forget the men who died here in a fight for freedom and

autonomy. Some visitors like to think the ghosts of the Texan dead may still inhabit these quiet gardens. The local tourist board claims that many of the heroes of the Alamo were buried in San Fernando Cathedral, a few block away, but no remains have been found.

Philipse Manor Hall
Yonkers, New York
c.1720

Miraculously unharmed by the spread of urban development, the Philipse Manor Hall in Yonkers is one of the most architecturally important houses of the Hudson valley: it may be one of the earliest examples of the Georgian style in colonial America and also provides a link with the Dutch colonial beginnings of the state of New York.

Although the present Manor Hall was built well after 1700 in Georgian style, at least part of its foundations may have been laid by Frederick Philipse, the former official carpenter of the Dutch West Indies Company, in the early 1680s. By this time, Philipse had made himself a large fortune in trade in New Amsterdam. In 1672 he began to buy land along the Hudson river, most of which had been held in the mid-17th century by an unsuccessful Dutch landowner, the Jonkheer Adriaen van der Donck (his title survives in the anglicized form, Yonkers).

Philipse is thought to have built his first house, for which stone was used, on his land in 1682, but since he received the royal charter granting him manorial rights in 1693, it is likely that he chose to build a more imposing manor house after this

date. The north wing of the present L-shaped Manor Hall is known to have been built in about 1745.

The south, shorter wing of the L, which has a facade built of rough gneiss rubble, is certainly much earlier than this, and may be the original house or, rather more likely, may have been built on the foundations of Philipse's first house. Of course, architectural historians would like the former possibility to be true, because this would make the south wing of the Philipse Manor Hall the first truly Georgian house to have been built in America. Sadly, however, it is more likely that the south wing dates from around 1719, when Frederick Philipse's son was married, or possibly even from 1725–30.

Whatever the date of its building, the Philipse Manor Hall, with its Classical entrance porch, modillioned cornice, hipped roof and balustraded deck, presents a very fine Georgian face to the world. Inside, the house possesses many equally noteworthy Georgian details, including a superb fireplace in the south-eastern parlour, flanked by Ionic columns, and a plastered ceiling covered with intricately detailed stucco moulding in an ornate Rococo style – something, if not unique, then certainly rare in America at that time.

Gonzales-Alvarez House
St. Augustine, Florida
c.1723

St. Augustine's Gonzales-Alvarez House – also known as the 'Oldest House' – may be older than the 1723 date attributed to it by historians. It may also be quite a bit younger, since extant

OPPOSITE: Philipse Manor Hall, Yonkers, New York.

documents discussing it do not go back as far as 1723. However, it is a fine example of the domestic architecture built by the Spanish in the 18th century and is worthy of its present role in the life of the city, which is as a museum devoted to St. Augustine's social history.

It is a simple, two-storey building. At ground-floor level it is built of the same coquina limestone that went into the walls of the Castillo de San Marcos (page 43 et seq.). The upper floor is of wooden frame construction, with clapboard coverings, and with porches at each end. A hipped roof covers the building.

Inside, visitors to the museum encounter the typical low ceilings, with cedar beams, of Spanish houses of the period. Large fireplaces dominate the living rooms, which have been cleverly and sympathetically furnished to show how the house, and the lives of people who lived there, changed with the passing generations, from its Spanish colonial days through the brief British occupation to post-Independence.

Shirley
Charles City County, Virginia
1723–38

This classic plantation house of the slave-owning South, on the banks of the James river, about halfway between Williamsburg and Richmond, was built by the Carters, one of Virginia's leading families. The plantation dates back to a patent granted in 1660 to Edward Hill, and the present mansion was built between 1723 and 1738 by John Carter and his wife, Elizabeth Hill Carter.

One of the largest and most impressive tidewater country

houses of its period, Shirley consisted of the main house flanked by two three-storey dependencies, probably connected to the main building by open passages. All three were built of brick. Visitors must have found Shirley an impressive sight when first they arrived at the house's landing stage on the river.

Inside, the main house had four rooms on each floor, while the principal feature of the great hall – unheated and with a sham fireplace purely for show – was its staircase. Thought to have been based on a staircase that appeared in William Halfpenny's *The Art of Sound Building* (published in London in 1725), the one at Shirley rose without apparent support in two long flights, the second of which was free-hanging.

John Carter died in 1742, and his widow lived on in the house for nearly 30 years. Their son, Charles Carter, did not come into full possession of the house until 1771, by which time it was so rundown that it was necessary for money to be spent on it. This was hardly of concern to Charles Carter, whose land holdings in Virginia spread over nine counties and were extensive enough to require nearly 800 slaves to work them.

Carter was a good businessman: for instance, he got out of tobacco and into wheat just in time, rightly foreseeing that the market for American tobacco would shrink if the British lost the Revolutionary War. He set about restoring Shirley, both inside and out, in the 1770s. Among the most noticeable of Charles Carter's innovations at Shirley were the two-storey porticoes, a popular Palladian-style motive in Virginia at that period, that he added on both the east and west facades. In the 1830s Carter's grandson replaced the steps and posts of these with porticoes in the Greek Revival style then popular in America.

Today, Shirley, still owned by the Carter family, attracts visitors for two reasons: it is a very fine plantation house and it was the childhood home of Ann Hill Carter, the mother of General Robert E. Lee, commander of the Confederate army of Northern Virginia in the American Civil War.

Madame John's Legacy
New Orleans, Louisiana
c.1727

The French, moving south along the Mississippi, which rises in Minnesota near the borders of Canada, first settled Louisiana in 1682, naming it after Louis XIV. They also founded New Orleans in 1718, as a trading outpost near the mouth of the Mississippi, naming it after the Duc d'Orléans, Regent of France. The buildings in the town that grew up round the trading post were constructed in an attractive mix of French and Creole architecture – a style that, nearly three centuries later, still gives the French Quarter of modern New Orleans its uniquely vibrant atmosphere.

Typical of this style is a house known as Madame John's Legacy, situated on Dumaine Street. Thought to be the oldest house in the French Quarter, it was built in typical French colonial style by a sea captain called Jean Pascal, who came to New Orleans in 1726. He built his house using the French *briquete-entre-poteaux* technique, which involved setting soft red brick between hand-hewn cypress beams. Slender cypress colonets were used to support the hipped roof, which had the double pitch characteristic of French New Orleans houses.

The house's walled-in basement, housing stuccoed brick

OPPOSITE: Shirley, Charles City County, Virginia.

Madame John's Legacy, New Orleans,
Louisiana.

pillars as well as office and service rooms, is a legacy of an earlier 'raised cottage' style, when houses in New Orleans were built on brick piers to raise them above possible floodwaters. At the main floor level, above the basement, the house has the light and airy wrap-around balcony, or *galerie*, typical of New Orleans style.

Jean Pascal's house was rebuilt after a fire in 1788 to be an exact replica of the original house. Its present name (there never was a Madame John) comes from a tragic short story by the 19th-century writer George Washington Cable, that achieved great popularity and helped attract thousands of visitors to New Orleans and to the house. Today, there are displays in the house concerning its history and inhabitants and a museum of Southern folk art.

Christ Church
Philadelphia, Pennsylvania
1727–54

Christ Church was built on the site of Philadelphia's first Anglican church, which had been built in 1695 in the town's first commercial area, near the riverfront, and enlarged in 1710–11. So rapid was the town's growth that the church soon became too small to accommodate comfortably its rapidly growing congregation. Fortunately for Christ Church, it numbered among its parishioners some of the most prominent people in the town, and they gave generously towards another enlarging and rebuilding programme which began in 1727.

The first stage involved a rebuilding of the west end of the church. Then in the 1730s the eastern two-thirds was replaced by the present building. Dr. John Kearsley supervised the building

Christ Church, Philadelphia, Pennsylvania.

programme, but the original drawings are lost, and it is not known how far, if at all, Kearsley influenced the actual design. Many details of the work were certainly taken from English books on architecture, and architectural historians have also noted a similarity to the church of St. Andrew-by-the-Wardrobe in London in Christ Church's general design.

By 1744, Philadelphia's new Christ Church, one of the largest and most ornate Georgian churches in the colonies, was complete. John Kearsley certainly did not have a hand in designing the steeple (records show the spire was built to the 'draft which Mr. Harrison drew' and was not completed until 1754). Details of its design may have come from another famous London church, St. Martin's-in-the-Fields.

If the exterior of the church (with its superimposed orders of pilasters and entablatures, and its great wooden balustrade topped with urns emitting carved flames) is too heavily ornate for some tastes, the interior, with its columns and arches separated by blocks of entablature verges on the pretentious, and is even harder to swallow. But Christ Church was important to Philadelphia and George Washington, Benjamin Franklin and Betsy Ross all worshipped here. So perhaps the restorers and redesigners of the 19th century could be forgiven for making the church look as grand as possible.

Independence Hall
Philadelphia, Pennsylvania
1732–53

Philadelphia's Independence Hall, or Old State House, as it was known in the years following its construction, was one of the outstanding buildings in a city known, like Boston, for the style and quality of its public works and institutions.

In 1730, the Provincial Assembly decided to have a State House constructed, and appointed a committee to undertake the work. After some deliberation, they chose a member of the committee and Speaker of the Assembly, Judge Andrew Hamilton, to look after the design. He had no experience of architecture, but had absorbed much of the basics of Georgian design while studying law at the Inns of Court in London.

Foundations were laid in 1731, and a team of brick-masons, marble workers, carpenters and joiners, plasterers, glaziers, woodcarvers and painters slowly and with many difficulties to overcome, including problems with the building, shortage of labour and not enough money, built Philadelphia's State House over the next 15 years. The Assembly met in its great room in 1736, despite there being no glazing in the windows and uncompleted plasterwork. By 1741 the second floor was finished and the roof was in place.

The assembly hall was finished and decorated in 1745, by which time Judge Hamilton was dead. The building's most distinctive feature, its great steeple tower, was completed by 1753, but in such a rickety manner that it had to be dismantled in 1781, and it was not until 1828 that Independence Hall's tower was restored. This time the architect was William Strickland, who knew how to go about building a tower that would last, and the construction is believed to have been executed by marine engineers from the South Philadelphia Arsenal. The tower, which was reinforced with diagonal girders, iron clamps and curved ships' knees as braces, remains in fine condition to this day.

Not that sightseers are too concerned with the state of the tower when visiting Independence Hall. Far more exciting is the thought that they are in the building where the Declaration of Liberty was prepared, signed and, after the ringing of the Liberty Bell, which hung in the hall, read out in public on 8 July 1776.

Van Cortlandt House
Bronx, New York, NY
1748

In the middle of the 18th century, Frederick van Cortlandt, a wealthy Dutch landowner, built himself a Georgian-style manor house on a wheat plantation on land originally settled by a Swede called Jonas Bronk, near the city the Dutch had built and named New Amsterdam. Today, that plantation is Van Cortlandt Park, in the heart of the Bronx, and Van Cortlandt House provides a vivid glimpse into the life of the descendants of New York's original Dutch settlers.

Frederick van Cortlandt was descended from an early Dutch settler, Oloff van Cortlandt, who made a fortune as a brewmeister in New Amsterdam, and whose manor in Croton-on-Hudson is now a living history museum. Frederick inherited his wealth and was connected or related to many of the most affluent families in New York. His house, built of rough stone, and with a basement, two main floors and dormer-windowed rooms in the roof, became a magnet for influential people – George Washington in particular, who used the house's dining room as one of his headquarters during the Revolutionary War.

The house remained in the family until the late 19th century, which was when the Bronx became part of New York proper. It

Opposite: Independence Hall, Philadelphia, Pennsylvania.

was also a time when immigrants of every nationality and religion were flooding into New York and, as it seemed to some, threatening the way of life of the original English and Dutch settlers. As a result, the National Society of Colonial Dames bought Van Cortlandt House, restored it to its mid-18th century glory, and opened it as the Van Cortlandt House Museum.

The visitor, having paused to examine the carved faces in the keystones of the windows, climbs the steps to the elegantly porticoed front door, and enters an 18th-century Dutch settler house, furnished in genuine period style. The parlour has its original 18th-century fittings, including wall cupboards and wooden window shutters, while the furniture is in period and there is a superb collection of blue Dutch delftware. One bedroom is furnished in 17th-century style. The whole house is a wonderfully evocative survival from New York's colonial past.

Spanish Governor's Palace
San Antonio, Texas
1749

'Palace' may be too grand a word for this simple, white-walled one-storey building, but since it was the home of a succession of Spanish officials during Texas's mission era, it is not too inappropriate. It was also built nearly 150 years later than the Governor's Palace at Santa Fe (page 34) and is therefore finer and more sophisticated in its construction.

The walls are stone, rather than adobe mud, and the entrance door is splendidly panelled and carved, its keystone bearing the arms of the Habsburgs and the date of the palace's construction. There are wrought-iron grilles, so typical of Spanish buildings,

over the windows, and drainpipes (*canales*) project from the walls to carry water from the roof away from the sides of the building.

Inside, the palace has ten rooms with flagstoned floors, low doorways and beamed ceilings. Two hooded fireplaces heated the ballroom, when the governor held winter receptions, while there was another in the white-walled dining room (*comedor*). There is a cobbled inner courtyard, with a large, covered portal. Today, the governor's well is a fountain shaded by lush palm trees.

OPPOSITE: Van Cortlandt House, Bronx, New York.

BELOW: Governor's Palace, San Antonio, Texas. Interior.

The Spanish Governor's Palace, San
Antonio, Texas. Interior.

The Spanish Governor's Palace was restored in the 1930s and is today maintained by the city of San Antonio as an attractive tourist site. With its many religious icons and wooden carvings giving it something of the atmosphere of a centuries-old church, the palace offers a glimpse into the lives of the civil and religious authorities, in what was once a remote outpost of Spain's American empire.

The Log Cabin

Contrary to the great 19th-century adage, 'from log cabin to White House', pioneers did not invent the log cabin. What is regarded as a uniquely home-grown contribution to American architectural style originated elsewhere, and specifically in northern Europe. In fact, it was Swedish settlers in Delaware in the first half of the 17th century who, having been accustomed

Pioneer log cabin, Salt Lake City, Utah.

to building log houses in their native land, introduced the
technique of building them to America.

Of course, by this time, other settlers, notably the British,
had been chopping down trees and building wooden houses,
helped, after about 1649, by the appearance of the first sawmills.
But their square-hewn logs, the ends cut to make dove-tailed or
lapped joints, made quite sophisticated buildings, requiring
tools, time, and skilled workmen to construct. But to build a log
cabin, all that was needed was an axe to cut down straight-
growing, slim trees, such as pine or spruce, and a few neighbours
to put the whole thing together.

Once cut, the logs were notched at the ends and laid
horizontally across each other at right angles, so that the log
ends protruded at the corners of the building. Any spaces
between the logs – and there may not have been any if the laying
of the logs together had been tightly done – could be filled, or
'clinked', with moss, clay or hardwood chips.

Although the Swedish settlements and trading posts in
Delaware did not survive independently for very long (New
Netherland swept them up in the 1650s and the British took over
a decade later), the Swedish themselves continued to live in the
region, building their log houses, though they also adapted their
techniques to suit what was being built around them.

Nothing seems to have survived from the earliest days of
Swedish settlement. The Swedish-built Lower Log House on
Darby Creek in Pennsylvania is a hewn-log house with fitted
corner joints. If it was built in 1640 – as it has been tentatively
dated – this house would be the oldest log building surviving in
America. The Lower Log House has two rooms, one bigger than
the other. There are corner fireplaces in each room, a placing
which makes a triangular-shaped flue, with two of its sides
formed by the walls of the house. A later, three-roomed Swedish
log house was adopted by so many settlers in Pennsylvania that
it was sometimes referred to as the 'Quaker' plan.

It tended to be Scottish and Irish settlers who took the log
cabin from the eastern states inland, moving west and south with
the frontier at a time when there were few sawmills but plenty of
trees. Early frontier log cabins were one-roomed and quite
primitive. They had earthen floors and the windows were
without glazing. As more space was needed by growing families,
a second room was added, usually in a back-to-back
arrangement, and with a central chimney stack serving both
rooms. In this 'saddle-bag' plan, rooms could not be very large
because their size was dictated by the length of the logs used in
the construction.

A step on from the saddle-bag cabin was the 'dog-run' or
'possum-trot' cabin. This had two separate rooms, each with its
own fireplace and linked by a breezeway in between. A single
roof covered all three elements of the dog-run cabin, with the
breezeway providing a pleasantly cool outdoor seating area in
the summer and a shelter for the dogs in winter.

OPPOSITE: An early miner's log cabin, Skagway, Alaska.

LEFT: Log cabin with chimney.

THE ARCHITECTURE OF INDEPENDENCE:
THE CLASSICAL INFLUENCE
c.1750–c.1820

CHAPTER TWO

THE ARCHITECTURE OF INDEPENDENCE: THE CLASSICAL INFLUENCE
c.1750–c.1820

RIGHT: Old State Capitol, Hartford,
Connecticut (1796). This is generally
believed to be the work of Charles
Bulfinch, and his first public building.

OPPOSITE: Monticello, Virginia, was
the home and personal creation of
Thomas Jefferson (see page 92).

The main architect, and some would say the 'only begetter'
of the Federal style of public building that superseded the
quietly confident and elegant Georgian architecture of pre-
Independence America, was Thomas Jefferson. He was a child
of the Age of Reason, which was a time when every educated
schoolboy could speak and read Latin and Greek, and when
important matters such as law, politics, invention and
architecture could be evaluated rationally, without emotion
being allowed to cloud the issue.

Sitting in his library, surrounded by his 6,000 books,
arguably the finest collection in America (and later to form the
foundation of the Library of Congress collection), Jefferson, in
the manner of an academic exercise, began to formulate a style
of architecture suited to a new and vibrant society. Even his
University of Virginia (page 115 et seq.) would not escape his
scrutiny: each of its halls of residence would be designed in a
different architectural style, making them of educational,
aesthetic as well as practical use to the students.

Such was the force of Jefferson's personality that his
proposals were accepted without demur by the new American
republic. His ideas and designs were for an architecture that
bypassed the Renaissance, and went directly back to that of
Classical Greece and Rome. European architects had been doing

84

OPPOSITE: The White House, Washington, DC, front view (see page 104).

the same thing, but it was in the United States of America that this new architectural Classicism took deepest root and lasted longest: for example, the West Building (page 123) of the country's National Art Gallery, that opened in Washington in 1941, is wholly Classical in its style.

The Neoclassical style of Federal architecture, that took its inspiration from both Greece and Rome, did not dispense with the Georgian influence completely – that happened when the Greek Revival style was established in the early decades of the 19th century; rather it took the Georgian house and public building and gave them a smoother, less domestically comfortable appearance.

In houses such as Washington's Mount Vernon (page 90 et seq.), brick outer walls were painted white, inside walls were made smooth with white-painted plaster, and any mouldings, especially on ceilings, were based on the quietly elegant work of the Adam brothers in England, themselves influenced by recent discoveries at Pompeii and Herculaneum in Italy. Front doors became the universally adopted 'Federal doorway', with narrow flanking sidelights and an elliptical fanlight, while the front porch evolved into a portico of increasing dominance.

In public buildings, however, the Classical assumed dominance over the Georgian style even more rapidly. Jefferson began the trend with his design for the Capitol in Richmond, Virginia (page 103), and continued it with his University of Virginia. What Jefferson had begun was continued by trained architects such as Benjamin Henry Latrobe and Charles Bulfinch, both of whom had learned their craft in England and Europe.

By 1799, the year in which he used the pure Ionic style

(echoing the Erechtheum in Athens) on the fine First Bank of Pennsylvania in Philadelphia, Latrobe, a trained engineer as well as architect, was being called the 'father of Greek Revival'. In the coming decades, he left his mark on public buildings as iconic as Washington's Capitol building (page 105 et seq.) and the Roman Catholic Cathedral in Baltimore (page 113).

While men like Latrobe and Bulfinch were bringing a new impetus to architecture in the eastern states, something very different was happening on the other side of the continent. In 1769, the year in which Thomas Jefferson was beginning to plan his Virginia country house, Monticello, the Spanish in California were establishing the last of their mission fields in America, 200 years after St. Augustine in Florida had been founded and 170 after the first of their New Mexican missions.

The chain of Spanish missions in California, evolutions of the Pueblo Indian-style missions of New Mexico, eventually numbered 21. They were built along the Camino Real, the royal road or 'king's highway', that stretched 500 miles (800km) from San Diego in the south to Sonoma, north of San Francisco Bay. Religion had less to do with the building of these missions than political expediency: the Spanish, well settled in Baja California, had decided to establish themselves in Alta California in the hope of forestalling any possible incursion into the region by Russians moving down the Pacific coast from Alaska.

In the South-West today, the hybrid Spanish/Pueblo-Indian style is the only one to have achieved a lasting influence in North America: it remains very much in vogue – as the Mission-Revival style in southern California and as the Pueblo style in the South-West (see pages 88, 89 and page 96 et seq.).

RIGHT & OPPOSITE: St. Xavier del Bac Mission, Tucson, Arizona.
There has been a mission on this site since 1692, founded by the Jesuit priest, Father Eusebio Francisco Kino. The building now standing was built in 1783, and was strongly influenced by Spanish architecture.

Jefferson's ideas grew even more ambitious once he had seen France, where he was American ambassador to the court at Versailles in the 1780s, and then England. Back in the United States in 1789, he began to remodel Monticello, virtually in homage to Palladio's rotunda-roofed Villa Capra (or Villa Rotonda, as it is known today) in Italy. He did not really finish tinkering with the design, adding bays and pavilions to his house and modifying them to achieve satisfactory visual effects, until 1809.

From the outside, standing on what Jefferson called a 'little mountain', looking towards the Blue Ridge Mountains, Monticello has the appearance of an elegant country house, its style clearly influenced by the villas of Palladio in northern Italy. But behind the symmetrical brick facade, with its central white Doric portico, balustraded pediment and octagonal dome over the hall, lies a house large enough to include extensive domestic quarters, wine and beer cellars (Jefferson made his own home brew but imported his wines from France), and stables built into a basement.

Inside, amid the Grecian motifs and detailing that Jefferson included as his interest in Classical Greek architecture increased, the light-filled house is full of oddly-shaped rooms, quirky details, clever contraptions and time-saving devices, such as dumb waiters that swing out of sight, gadgets for opening shutters, and Jefferson's bed set in an alcove with doors on either side, so that he could save time by getting out of whatever side of his bed led directly to dressing room or study, where the elaborate dual-pen device that Jefferson designed to make automatic copies of all his letters can still be seen. Another

OPPOSITE, LEFT & PAGE 96:
Monticello, home of Thomas Jefferson, and his own architectural creation.

PAGE 97: The Mission Santa Barbara, founded by Father Fermin Francisco de Lasuén in 1786, who arrived in San Diego, California, with Father Junípero Serra and later succeeded him as padre presidente.

clever gadget, still in the house, is the dial connected to the weather vane on the portico, which allowed him to know which way the wind was blowing without having to go outside.

Familiar to every American today, because it is on the back of the nickel coin, Monticello is a brilliant evocation of plantation life in pre-Civil War Virginia. The house sits amid flower and vegetable gardens in extensive grounds, where the remains of its slave quarters, Mulberry Row, vie for attention with Jefferson's grave, marked by a simple stone obelisk in a grove of ancient hardwood trees.

Spanish Missions in California 1769–1823

Father Junípero Serra, the Franciscan friar chosen by the Spanish to head their missionary work in California, founded his first mission, San Diego de Alcala, at San Diego, site of the first Spanish presidio or fortress, in July 1769. That mission established, Scrra and Gaspar de Portolá, the Spanish governor, headed north to Monterey Bay. Here, surrounded by the immense beauty of the Monterey peninsula, a wooden cross was erected on the shore, a bell was hung from the branch of an oak tree, and the first Mass was said. These ceremonials became the regular way of establishing a mission from then on.

The second Spanish mission, San Carlos Borromeo (Carmel), was founded at Monterey in June 1770, at the same time that the Spanish flag was unfurled over the new presidio. In the coming years, another 19 missions were established along the Camino Real, a 500-mile road between San Diego in

RIGHT & OPPOSITE: The Mission Santa
Barbara, California.

the south and Sonoma in the north, with each mission just a day's ride or hard walk from the next.

Each mission was a whole community with a church at its heart, and all were augmented, rebuilt and restored over the years. Precise layouts differed from mission to mission, but most consisted of a large quadrangle of buildings, the largest of which was the church, surrounding an open patio or courtyard. Entry to the mission was by way of a gate set between two buildings on one side of the quadrangle. The mission churches were not oriented in a particular direction: San Diego faces south-east, San Carlos north-east, and Santa Barbara south.

A much greater variety of materials and range of structural systems were used in the California missions than in those of New Mexico. Adobe, a mixture of clay, sand and water, sometimes with straw added as a binder, remained the chief building material. It was sun-dried in large blocks and laid with mud- or lime-mortar joints. A layer of lime-and-sand stucco protected the walls from erosion due to weather.

The Spanish missions in California flourished for over 100 years. Eventually, when they were secularized under Mexican rule in 1834, much of their land was given, not to the local American Indians, but to Spanish-speaking ranchers. The Americans entered Monterey to claim California in 1846, the year the last padre-presidente of the Spanish missions died. Later, both presidents Lincoln and Buchanan tried to invalidate Mexican sales contracts and restore at least some of the land to the missions, but it was not nearly enough to revive them.

RIGHT: The Mission Santa Barbara, with its twin bell towers.

OPPOSITE: The Franciscan Mission of San Luis Rey, Oceanside, California, founded in 1798 by Father Fermin Francisco de Lasuén, successor of Father Junípero Serra.

Of the California missions restored in the 20th century, those well worth a visit include:

Carmel: the Carmel Mission Basilica has three small museums in the mission compound, tracing the history of the second and, some say, the most romantic of the Spanish missions in California.

San Antonio de Padua and San Purisima: excellent reconstruction and restoration at these two missions give a good sense of what early settler and mission life was like.

San Juan Capistrano: famous for the migrating swallows it welcomes every March.

San Luis Rey: this was the largest and most populous settlement, made particularly famous by Thornton Wilder's novel, *The Bridge of San Luis Rey*. The mission's huge *lavanderia*, or washing area, is now a fine sunken garden.

Santa Barbara: The Mission Santa Barbara, in the hills above the town, is known as 'the queen of missions'. Its church, with a twin-towered facade combining Romanesque and Spanish Mission styles, was built to replace three earlier adobe mission churches destroyed by earthquakes, and was completed in 1820. Today, a small museum displays items from the mission's archives, but cannot do more than give a hint of what life was like in the old mission, with its great system of aqueducts, waterworks, mills, pottery kiln and much besides.

State Capitol
Richmond, Virginia
1788–98

Richmond became Virginia's state capital in 1780, during the American Revolution (1775–83). The Virginians, mindful of Williamsburg's vulnerability to British attack, moved their capital 50 miles (80km) inland. After the war, during which time Richmond was twice put to the torch, the city was rebuilt in grand style, the new State Capitol being the grandest building of all.

The greatest influence in the design and building of the State Capitol was Thomas Jefferson, as was the case with many of the state's great buildings. His inspiration was the Maison Carrée, built by the Romans in the first century BC in Nîmes in the south of France. Jefferson had visited this superb Corinthian-columned temple during his time as American ambassador in France, and he was still in France when he designed Richmond's new Capitol. He seems to have had the classical splendour of Ancient Rome in mind as early as 1776, the year he drew up the act transferring the state capital to Richmond. In it, he specified that land be set aside for the construction of public buildings 'in a handsome manner with walls of brick or stone, and Porticos... and with pillars and pavements of stone'.

Jefferson had some help in the design of Virginia's State Capitol. His collaborator was the French Neoclassical architect and author of influential books, Charles-Louis Clérisseau (1721–1820). The Capitol was built on a larger scale than the Maison Carrée and its columns were Ionic rather than the more decorative Corinthian, smooth rather than fluted. The greater

OPPOSITE: The State Capitol, Richmond, Virginia, the work of Thomas Jefferson with Charles-Louis Clérisseau.

The White House, Washington, DC.

size was necessary because the building was to contain both houses of the legislature as well as administrative offices. Not visible from the outside was a domed central rotunda.

This building was not only a pioneering exercise in reviving the Classical architecture of Rome in the new United States, it also pre-dated by decades the reuse of the Classical temple form in European architecture. It became an exemplar for

official buildings of all kinds, both in the United States and the wider world.

The State Capitol is the focal point of Richmond today, visible on its hill from all over the city. It has been in continuous use since 1788 as the seat of the state government. Inside, under the domed rotunda, is the only marble statue of George Washington modelled from life, while busts of Thomas Jefferson and the seven other Virginia-born American presidents line the Capitol's walls.

The White House
Washington, DC
1792–1829

The White House, situated on Pennsylvania Avenue in Washington, DC, and the official residence of the President of the United States of America, was designed in the Palladian manner by an Irish immigrant architect, James Hoban (1762–1831). His 1792 designs for the White House were modelled on the Georgian manor houses of Dublin, with which he was most familiar, and featured oval rooms, giving future American presidents their famous Oval Office; rooms like these were copied in other American country houses of the period.

Hoban's White House was completed in the Neoclassical style in 1800, though the familiar curved porticoes were not added until 1807–08. They were the work of the great Federal-period architect, Benjamin H. Latrobe, by this time fully in command of his position as 'father of the Greek Revival' in America.

Incumbent presidents made their own mark on the buildings

right from the beginning: Thomas Jefferson, as had been the case at Monticello, made his additions in a practical way, adding the first lavatories in the White House. This was just before the British severely damaged the building during the war of 1812. The White House was quickly rebuilt, in the same style as before its near-destruction, but extensions were very soon needed, and this continued to be the case right through the 19th century.

By mid-20th century, the White House's constant additions, often effected at speed, had rendered the building so fragile that Harry S. Truman, president at the time, had to move out for four years while a modern steel frame was inserted into the structure. Truman's own contribution to the White House was a balcony added to the south-side portico. Despite its central role in the life of the nation, the White House remains, at heart, a not very large and quite homely country house – a suitable residence for the nation's First Family.

United States Capitol
Washington, DC
1792–1830; 1851–63

It is rather misleading to assign dates to the building of the United States Capitol. It is one of the most impressive of all the palace-like government buildings in Neoclassical style, built throughout the Western world and beyond in the 18th and 19th centuries, and evolved over many decades of enlargement and modification. The two sets of dates above simply indicate two periods when building work was particularly concentrated.

George Washington laid the foundation stone for the

United States Capitol, Washington, DC.

nation's new Capitol in 1793, and thereafter a succession of influential architects were involved in its design and construction. An English-born physician, William Thornton, won the design competition for the Capitol in 1792, and with the help of a French architect, E.S.H. Hallet, produced something that was really a Palladian country house at heart and in keeping with the style introduced by Thomas Jefferson. Thornton never oversaw the building of his design, which proceeded rather slowly. The Senate Wing, its construction supervised by the designer of the White House, James Hoban, was completed in 1800.

Things progressed rather more rapidly when Benjamin Henry Latrobe (1764–1820) took over in 1803, and the House of Representatives wing was finished by 1811, complete with Latrobe's semicircular hall with its Corinthian colonnades, which, in a neat reference to his adopted country, dispensed with the more usual acanthus leaves and were given maize instead. In 1814 the British came up the Potomac and burned much of Washington down, including the Capitol and the White House. Latrobe, after making some revisions in the light of experience gained in his first years of work, began rebuilding the Capitol. The work was completed in 1830, by which time Charles Bulfinch, builder of the Massachusetts State House (page 108), was overseeing the work.

By the middle of the 19th century, Congress had outgrown its home, and between 1851 and 1863 the whole complex was rebuilt, in marble instead of the original sandstone, and on a much greater scale, to a design in the Greek Revival style by Thomas U. Walter (1804–87). This was when the Capitol

OPPOSITE & LEFT: The Capitol, Washington, DC.

PAGES 108 & 109: Massachusetts State House, Boston.

received its extensive wings and its massive 224-ft (68-m) dome, which has been described as 'an offspring of St. Paul's Cathedral' in London – accurate enough as far as the design goes, but for the fact that its cast-iron shell puts it firmly in the 19th century.

A century later, in 1960, the Capitol's east facade was lengthened by another 33ft (10m), while at the same time Walter's great dome was topped by a 20-ft (6-m) statue depicting Armed Freedom. Today, the statue rises above a vast complex of ornate chambers and committee rooms, grand halls and public spaces, much of them packed with monuments and statues recording the achievements of past leaders of the nation – all of them busy with the affairs of the world's most powerful state.

Massachusetts State House
Boston, Massachusetts
1795–97

The present meeting house of the State of Massachusetts, built in Boston in 1795–97, was the work of an up-and-coming architect of the day, Charles Bulfinch (1763–1844). He had a great deal to live up to, for the Second Town House, which it replaced, had seen many of Boston's most momentous events during the 18th century.

But Charles Bulfinch had learned his business in Europe, especially in England, where he had absorbed the work of the brothers Robert and James Adam. After he returned to Boston in 1786, still in his 20s, Bulfinch became one of the most influential architects of the day, helping to popularize the Neoclassical Federal style that ousted the Georgian from the

altered in 1860, 1898, 1903, 1907, 1915, 1917 and 1956. After City Hall became the focus of New York's reception of the aviator Charles Lindburgh in 1927, it became the traditional focus for ticker-tape parades for all kinds of American hero, from astronauts to sports stars. The steps outside City Hall have long been a popular place for demonstrations and public press conferences by politicians, including the Mayor of New York.

City Hall certainly has character and style, which were acknowledged in 1966, when the Hall's exterior was given designated status, followed by its interior in 1976. City Hall was thus saved from developers, intent on obtaining a piece of immensely valuable real estate at the heart of downtown Manhattan.

Roman Catholic Cathedral
Baltimore, Maryland
1805–21

Founded as a Catholic colony, the first in the new, strongly Protestant America, Maryland was also the first state to build a Roman Catholic cathedral. The building of the cathedral in Baltimore, the state's largest city and main port, was the Catholic Church in America's way of celebrating its post-Independence religious freedom, and John Carroll, the country's first Catholic bishop and later Archbishop of Baltimore, deemed it right and fitting that it should be built in the forward-looking Neoclassical architectural style of the Federal capital, Washington.

Work on Baltimore's cathedral – the Basilica of the National Shrine of the Assumption of the Blessed Virgin Mary, to give it

LEFT & PAGE 114: Roman Catholic Cathedral, Baltimore, Maryland.

The National Gallery of Art: The West Building (1937–41)

Since the site chosen for the nation's national art gallery was at the foot of the Capitol, in the National Mall, in the heart of the federal capital, as it had been planned by Pierre Charles L'Enfant in the 18th century, it was probably inevitable that John Russell Pope (1874–1937) should maintain the Neoclassical tradition of Washington's public buildings in the design of the gallery, planned for the mid 20th century.

The gift of industrialist Andrew Mellon to the American people, the National Gallery of Art's original building (now called the West Building) is firmly and uncompromisingly Palladian. With one appalling world war not long over and another looking more and more likely in Europe as he worked, perhaps Pope (who died in 1937) preferred to look back for inspiration to a time when the new United States of America, inspired by such giants as Thomas Jefferson, took as its architectural model the democratic values of Ancient Greece.

There is no denying, however, that the West Building of the National Galley of Art, the Mall facade of which spreads, windowless, to either side of a marble pedimented portico supported on Ionic columns, may be visually stunning but it does have the air of a building coolly indifferent to the world around it. The mid 20th century seems a little late to be designing buildings with such formal, uncompromising – and rather lifeless – Neoclassical correctness. The interior is a very different matter, for John Russell Pope ensured that exhibition rooms in the West Building would be harmonious settings for the works of art displayed in them, the details of their design reflecting the period and country in which the art was produced.

The National Gallery of Art: The East Building (1968–78)

Within 20 years of John Russell Pope's building being completed, the National Gallery of Art began to think about a second building, which would house much of the gallery's growing collection of 20th-century art. To the east of Pope's building was a difficult, 9-acre (4-hectare) trapezoidal site,

OPPOSITE & BELOW: National Gallery of Art (West Building), Washington DC, the work of architect John Russell Pope.

actually inscribed on L'Enfant's original plan. Born in China in 1917, the American-educated Ieoh Ming Pei, who had had his own office in New York since the mid-1950s, won the commission to design the new art gallery building.

To fit the constraints of the site, Pei designed a building consisting of two complementary triangles connected by a triangular central garden courtyard. In its location, its scale and its material (pink-hued Tennessee marble) Pei's building related closely to Pope's, but in every other way it did not. Pei's East Building was conceived as a piece of hard-edged 1960s sculpture, its volumes configured in strongly geometrical terms. This abstract style was, in fact, well suited to the site – and to the abstract art that made up much of the work displayed in the building's three diamond-shaped gallery spaces. Each of these spaces, or pods, had its own skylight, stairs and lift and were linked by long-spanned gallery bridges.

Pei extended the use of the marble of the facade and the entrance plaza paving into the central garden court, the building's main focal and circulating point, as a way of integrating the whole scheme. Dominating the courtyard and giving it a wonderful airy lightness, was an insulated-glass skylight with an aluminium sunscreen. The skylight's welded steel frame, composed of glazed tetrahedrons, foreshadowed the glass pyramids over the grand entrance to the Louvre museum in Paris that were to make I.M. Pei's name familiar around the world later in the decade.

OPPOSITE & LEFT: National Gallery of Art (East Building), Washington, DC, by I.M. Pei.

CHAPTER THREE

GREEK REVIVAL & VICTORIAN ECLECTICISM
1820s–c.1914

Second Bank of the U.S., Philadelphia, Pennsylvania

Beauregard-Keyes House, New Orleans, Louisiana

Merchants' Exchange, Philadelphia, Pennsylvania

Henry B. Clarke House, Chicago, Illinois

Old Courthouse Museum, St. Louis, Missouri

Trinity Church, New York, NY

Houmas House, nr. Burnside, Louisiana

Lyndhurst, Tarrytown, New York

Girard College, Philadelphia, Pennsylvania

Gallier House, New Orleans, Louisiana

Parliament Buildings, Ottawa, Ontario, Canada

St. Patrick's Cathedral, New York, NY

Second Presbyterian Church, Chicago, Illinois

Trinity Church, Boston, Massachusetts

Boston Public Library, Boston, Massachusetts

Banff Springs Hotel, Banff, Alberta, Canada

Biltmore, Asheville, North Carolina

Marshall Field Store, Chicago, Illinois

Pierpont Morgan Library, New York, NY

Grand Central Rail Terminal, New York, NY

Pennsylvania Station, New York, NY

U.S. Custom House, New York, NY

CHAPTER THREE
GREEK REVIVAL & VICTORIAN ECLECTICISM
1820s–c.1914

RIGHT: St. Patrick's Cathedral, New York, an example of Gothic Revival architecture (see page 156).

OPPOSITE: One of the 30 eclectic buildings, this one modelled in the Classical style, that make up McGill University, Montreal, Quebec, founded in 1821.

PAGE 130: Philadelphia City Hall, Philadelphia, Pennsylvania (1871–1901), built in the French Second Empire style to a design of John McArthur.

PAGE 131: Nottoway Plantation, New Orleans, Louisana. Built in 1852 in the Greek Revival style.

During most of the middle decades of the 19th century, in America as in Europe, 'anything goes' became a guiding principle for architects and designers responding to the many dramatic changes in taste and artistic sensibilities of the age. During the Federal period of the later 18th century, of course, other styles could also be discerned: even the scholarly Classicist Thomas Jefferson, though his Monticello was created in a Neoclassical style, erected amusing Gothic and Chinese pavilions in the gardens of his house. When the Rationalism that had guided thinking for much of the 18th century gave way to Romanticism, architectural horizons began to broaden dramatically.

The Greek Revival style dominated American architecture from about 1820 to mid-century. A more refined version of ancient Greek architecture than the Federal Neoclassical architecture of Jefferson's time, the Greek Revival style became de rigueur for public buildings and business enterprises, private houses from New England to Louisiana, and churches, including America's first Roman Catholic cathedral in Baltimore and the First Presbyterian Church in Tallahassee, Florida.

Even when it had become the most dominant style in American architecture, Greek Revival did not have the architectural landscape entirely to itself: among its earliest

challengers was that based on the Gothic style of medieval England and Europe. Architects in America adopted the picturesque, less rational Gothic style as an antidote to the rather austere Greek Revival which, after all, had pagan origins. Gothic had been the inspiration for some of the greatest Christian churches and cathedrals in Europe, and was therefore already familiar to the growing numbers of immigrants crossing the Atlantic and making their home in America. It is not surprising, therefore, that Gothic was the style chosen for New York's famous Trinity Church (page 144), and also for the Second Presbyterian Church in Chicago (page 159), the fastest-growing city in America in the mid 19th century.

Even architects renowned for their work in the Greek Revival style also designed in Gothic and other styles. Benjamin Latrobe's early designs for his Catholic cathedral in Baltimore (page 113) included one with a strongly Gothic line, while William Strickland, designer of the superb Greek Revival Merchants' Exchange in Philadelphia (page 139), also created a Gothic Masonic Temple in Philadelphia (1809) and an Egyptian-looking First Presbyterian Church in Nashville (1848).

Romanesque, even earlier than Gothic, and Renaissance were two other European styles that found enthusiastic supporters among North American architects. Henry Hobson Richardson, one of several American architects to study at the École des Beaux-Arts in Paris, was influential in introducing the Romanesque style to American architects. It was used in buildings as different as the rapidly growing McGill University in Montreal (page 129), founded in 1821, its campus now totalling 30 buildings in a richly eclectic range of styles, and

RIGHT: Biltmore, Asheville, North Carolina (see page 171).

OPPOSITE: Banff Springs Hotel, Banff National Park, Alberta, Canada (see page 164 et seq.).

Grand Central Rail Terminus in New York (page 175 et seq.).

To a large extent, the Romanesque and Renaissance styles overlapped with the more Classically ornamented Beaux-Arts style, and all three were introduced to the trainee architects of Europe and America who studied at the influential École des Beaux-Arts in Paris. The Beaux-Arts style, with its emphasis on the importance of the various components of a building being as well proportioned as the structure itself, became a major force in American architecture after the Civil War. It also influenced the design of many buildings, from great houses such as Biltmore in North Carolina (page 171) and the Marshall Field Store in Chicago (page 172) to many of America's first skyscrapers.

An underlying reason for this eclecticism in American architecture in the 19th century was the changing perception of the role of the architect in American society. At the beginning of the 19th century, architects were only just beginning to convince clients that, rather than being master-builders, they were professional designers, and should have full control of all aspects of their buildings' construction. By 1857, the year in which the American Institute of Architects was founded, architects had become people of standing and influence in society, able to persuade their patrons and clients that the ideas and styles they were paying architects to deliver were more than justified by the end results.

OPPOSITE: The Renaissance Revival Austin State Capitol, Austin, Texas (1882–88). Architect: Elijah E. Myers.

LEFT: City Hall, San Francisco, California (completed in 1915). Architect: Arthur Brown Jr.

Second Bank of the U.S.
Philadelphia, Pennsylvania
1817–24

Benjamin H. Latrobe, king of the Greek Revival in America in the early 19th century, was responsible for the design of this bank, as he had been for another in Philadelphia, the Bank of Pennsylvania, built in 1799.

Latrobe had fronted his design of 1799 (later demolished) with a six-columned portico in Greek Ionic style and had given it a domed banking hall. Now, in conscious imitation of the Parthenon on the Acropolis in Athens, he gave the front facade of the new building of the recently incorporated Second Bank of the U.S., a superb Doric-columned pedimented portico.

The Parthenon was very much in the news at this time, because the British Lord Elgin, seeing the dilapidated state of the temple's marble frieze, had bought large parts of it for a considerable sum from its Turkish owners and transported them back to England between 1803 and 1812. When displayed in London, the Elgin Marbles caused a sensation, but whether or not Latrobe took his inspiration from them, his design for the new bank in Philadelphia has been described as one of the finest examples of the Greek Revival in the United States.

Not long after the Second Bank of the U.S. moved into its new building, its president, Nicholas Biddle, was involved in a bitter quarrel with President Andrew Jackson: the bank ceased to exist in 1836, when the president vetoed the bill renewing its charter. From 1845 until 1935, the building was the Philadelphia Custom House, and today it is one of the listed buildings in Philadelphia's Independence National Historic Park and the

OPPOSITE & LEFT: Second Bank of the
United States, Philadelphia,
Pennsylvania.

Beauregard-Keyes House, New

Orleans, Louisiana.

home of the 'People of Independence' exhibition. Behind that superb Doric portico is a collection of 185 paintings, many of them by Charles Wilson Peale, of leaders of the colonial and federal periods, military officers, scientists and explorers

Beauregard-Keyes House
New Orleans, Louisiana
1826

This house, named after two of its most famous residents, is also of interest architecturally, because it was one of the earliest houses largely built in the Greek Revival style in New Orleans. Sited in the heart of the historic French Quarter, it successfully merged the Creole style of Lousiana with the Greek Revival popular in states further north, but uncommon in the French Quarter, where most houses were built and furnished in a simple French colonial style.

The Beauregard-Keyes house was built by a wealthy auctioneer, Joseph Le Carpentier, in 1826. It was a New Orleans 'raised cottage' type of building, with a basement at ground-floor level, Doric columns at balcony level and twin staircases. It also had a rear courtyard and separate slave quarters, a common feature of antebellum houses in Louisiana.

Like most houses in the close-packed French Quarter, where fire was a major hazard, the Beauregard-Keyes house had its kitchen built outside the main house. It also had another common feature – indoor plumbing – made possible by a cistern that either collected water from the rooftop or from the river (in which case river sediment was allowed to settle before the water was used).

And the two famous residents? The first was the Civil War general, Pierre G.T. Beauregard. General Beauregard won his place in American history when he gave the order to fire on Fort Sumter in Charleston, South Carolina, thus beginning the Civil War. He and several members of his family rented the house for 18 months in 1865–67.

The second famous person to live there was the author Francis Parkinson Keyes, the house being her summer residence from 1944 until her death in 1970. She set several of her 51 novels in New Orleans, including *Dinner at Antoine's* (1948), set round the famous New Orleans restaurant, dating back to around 1840 and still full of old-world charm; *Steamboat Gothic* (1952); and *Madame Castel's Lodger* (1962), which was set in the Beauregard-Keyes House at the time of General Beauregard's residence.

Mrs Keyes left her house to a foundation which opens the house (which is full of Mrs Keyes' furnishings), the rear buildings and the garden to the public. Happily, the house was not badly damaged during Hurricane Katrina in September 2005.

Merchants' Exchange
Philadelphia, Pennsylvania
1832–34

This stunning example of the Greek Revival style was America's first stock exchange. From Philadelphia's earliest days, the city's merchants, traders and shipping magnates were in the habit of gathering together in a succession of coffee houses to discuss the business of the day. In the 1770s a group of wealthy businessmen set up the Merchants' Coffee House,

Merchants' Exchange, Philadelphia, Pennsylvania.

soon renamed the City Tavern, which, for 50 years was the hub of commercial life in Philadelphia.

By 1831, the City Tavern had become too small, and could no longer be used as a meeting place. So a group of men, led by the immensely wealthy banker, Stephen Girard, decided to establish a society for the building of an exchange, and a rising local architect called William Strickland (1788–1854), already known for his work on Independence Hall, the U.S. Naval Asylum and the U.S. Mint, was chosen to design and build it.

Strickland was given a difficult corner site on South 3rd Street at Walnut and Dock Streets in the historic heart of Philadelphia. Dock Street was one of the few curved streets in Philadelphia's famed grid-type layout, because it followed the line of Dock Creek, an inlet of the Delaware river that had been paved over. But difficulties seemed to bring out the best and most innovative in Strickland: we have already seen (in Chapter One) how in 1828 he solved the problem of the steeple that should have topped Independence Hall, but which had been so rickety that it was removed and not replaced for 50 years.

Now, he chose to build the Merchants' Exchange on a line that followed the curve of Dock Street at basement level, from the second storey of which rose a semicircular portico with six Corinthian columns. A flight of steps at either side of the building, each guarded by a recumbent lion on a plinth – brought from Italy and the gift of a local merchant in 1838 – rose to the second-floor entrance. Strickland decorated the lip of the portico with a sculptured Minoan design and, possibly mindful of an enthusiastic 1831 newspaper description of

Philadelphia as 'truly the Athens of America', topped the building with a tower adapted from the design of the Choragic Monument of Lysicrates in Athens.

Today, Strickland's Merchants' Exchange, which has not been the city's stock exchange for a century, is not open to the public. Since 1952, Philadelphia's Independence National Historic Park has owned and maintained the building, and it is one of the architectural highlights of a walk through the park. Since this 45-acre (18-hectare) park, which has been dubbed 'America's most historic square mile', also contains Independence Hall, 'birthplace of American government', Carpenters' Hall, site of the First Continental Congress in 1774, and the Liberty Bell Pavilion, Strickland's Merchants' Exchange has some very impressive buildings to keep it company.

Henry B. Clarke House (Widow Clarke House) Chicago, Illinois
1836

When this house was built at 18th and Wabush in the mid 1830s, it was right at the outer limits of Chicago's built-up area. This was the decade, however, in which Chicago was beginning to expand rapidly: between 1830 and 1870 the population of the then small settlement on a stretch of marshy land smelling of wild onion grew from only 100 to nearly 300,000, and soon Henry Clarke's house was surrounded by new buildings. By the early 20th century it was actually within calling distance of Millonaires' Row and the mansions of the seriously rich.

The house's architect is not known. It is possible he had come west to Chicago from the eastern states, bringing with him all the latest romantic thinking on architecture, with its emphasis on the Greek Revival and Romanesque styles. But whoever designed the house (perhaps it was Henry B. Clarke himself) had experience of other kinds of houses, too, so it is a splendidly confident mixture of several domestic styles.

The design of this white-painted clapboard house, with its shingle roof, is basically Greek Revival, as its entrance facade pediment, with the round window at its centre, indicates. In contrast, the central roof tower suggests the house's designer had noted, and liked, the details of the Romanesque style. Instead of a cellar, the house has a basement, which necessitated the building of a tall flight of steps up to the front door. The Georgian-looking windows at the entrance level are tall, rectangular sash windows with divider bars, and contrast interestingly with the arched windows (again, more Romanesque then Greek Revival) in the tower.

The Henry B. Clarke House was fortunate enough to be in that part of Chicago that survived the great fire of 1871 that destroyed nearly two million dollars-worth of property, including nearly the whole business section, and left almost 100,000 people homeless. It also survived the Depression, when the millionaires moved away from this part of town and the neighbourhood began to decline. For many years the Clarke House was a community centre.

When the Prairie Avenue Historic District was established, this one remaining house from Chicago's early pioneering days was moved the short distance to 1855 South Indiana Avenue,

OPPOSITE: Old Courthouse Museum, St. Louis, Missouri.

RIGHT: Interior view of dome.

where it is now a small museum and one of the highlights of the Historic District. Another highlight is the Glessner House, a stone Romanesque construction built in 1887. It is the only house designed by Henry Hobson Richardson to survive in Chicago and is now a museum, full of furniture and William Morris fabrics and wallpapers in the Arts and Crafts style.

Old Courthouse Museum, St. Louis, Missouri
1839–62

Sometimes a building proves to have been such a perfect architectural setting for events destined to take place there in the future, that a degree of precognition seems possible. This certainly applies to the courthouse, built in serene, quietly Classical Greek Revival style in St. Louis in the 1840s.

After it became part of the United States, as a result of the Louisiana Purchase of 1803, the French-founded town of St. Louis became an important staging post for wagons moving westward across the Great Plains. It never quite lost its European air, so when a courthouse was planned for the growing city, it was appropriate that the still highly fashionable Greek Revival style should be used.

The St. Louis courthouse, complete with its simple, pedimented entrance portico, with a great central dome towering above, had only been open a couple of years when it became the scene of two of the most constitutionally important trials ever to take place in an American court. These were the trials that grew out of the Dred Scott case, held in 1847 and 1850.

Trinity Church, Manhattan, New York.

Dred Scott was a black slave who argued that because his owner had taken him to two non-slave states, where he had lived and worked for some time, he had the right to be set free. Two years after his case was upheld in 1850, it went on appeal to the Supreme Court, which decided that Scott, having been born a slave in a slave state, was a chattel that his master could take, like any other chattel, anywhere he liked. This decision, which meant, in effect, that the Constitution of the United States saw slaves as legitimate personal property, sent shock waves through America, and is now seen as one of the major causes of the Civil War.

The importance of the Dred Scott trials ensured that when the Old Courthouse was turned into a museum in the 20th century, the two courtrooms where the trials took place would be restored. They are now major attractions in the museum, even though most of the other exhibits and displays are devoted to the history of St. Louis and the settling of the West.

Trinity Church
Manhattan, New York, NY
1839–46

One of America's oldest Anglican parishes was founded in Lower Manhattan in 1697. In the early 1830s, by which time the Anglican Church in America had been renamed Episcopal, it was decided to replace the parish church on Broadway at Wall Street (the second one there since 1698). An English-born architect settled in Boston called Richard Upjohn (1802–78) was chosen to design the new church.

Upjohn, who had departed from the Greek Revival style of many of his contemporaries, designed a new Trinity Church, that soared above New York in impressive Gothic style. Upjohn's church was built in the rosy sandstone known to New Yorkers as brownstone, and had the buttresses, finials and high, narrow arched windows typical of the clean-lined Decorated and Early Perpendicular styles of English Gothic (late 13th and 14th centuries). Its octagonal spire on a square tower reaching 280ft (85m) into the sky, made Trinity Church New York's tallest building for half a century and marked the beginning of a great age of building in the Gothic Revival style in America.

To reach the interior of Trinity Church, the visitor passes through splendid sculpted brass doors, inspired by the great Ghiberti Doors of Paradise on Florence Cathedral and designed by Richard Morris Hunt. Inside, the light filters through fine stained glass, thought to be some of the earliest used in American churches, that includes a window depicting Christ and the Saints, rising above the altar at the east end of the long, narrow nave.

Trinity Church stands in a churchyard that miraculously, given its situation, has the sequestered air typical of an English churchyard. Since many prominent New Yorkers were members of Trinity parish, it is not surprising that there should be some very famous names on its monuments and gravestones. Alexander Hamilton, the first U.S. Secretary of the Treasury (his face is on the ten-dollar bill), who was killed in a duel with the then Vice-President Aaron Burr, is buried here, not far from Robert Fulton, the inventor of the steamboat, and William Bradford, who founded New York's first newspaper in 1725.

Richard Upjohn, who became famous for his Gothic churches, was the founder and first president of the American Institute of Architects. He would be proud that today, far from being diminished by the towering skyscrapers of New York's financial district that hem it in, Trinity Church remains a symbol of the survival power of Christian faith and spirituality in a troubled and dangerous world.

Houmas House
nr. Burnside, Louisiana
c.1840

A 'River Road' runs along the east bank of the Mississippi river between New Orleans and Baton Rouge, Louisiana's state capital since 1849. Along the way are many large plantation houses, built during the years when Louisiana's wealth was based on sugar. Some, like the comparatively unassuming Laura Plantation at Vacherie, are built in the relatively simple French Creole style; others, like the dramatically sited Oak Alley Plantation, a little upriver from Laura, are large Greek Revival-style temples to wealth and position built by American settlers following the Louisiana Purchase in 1803.

Houmas House, named after the Native American Houma people, who were displaced from their lands in the Cajun Wetlands by the Acadians in the mid 19th century, lies on the east bank of the Mississippi, upriver from the Sunshine Bridge and Burnside. It is a fine example of the Greek Revival style of plantation home built in Louisiana from the early 19th century.

The house, once the focal point of a large sugar plantation, was first built in the 1790s, and is now only the back

PAGE 146: Houmas House, near Burnside, Louisiana.

PAGE 147: Lyndhurst, Tarrytown, New York.

end of a large, two-storey stuccoed brick house, built around 1840. It is surrounded by a graceful, smooth-columned portico, with an elegantly balustraded balcony at second-floor level. The tall sash windows on both floors have shutters, and there are tall, narrow dormer windows in the roof. Beyond the house are hexagonal garçonnières—outbuilding accommodation for the sons of the family.

Houmas House avoided damage during the Civil War because its owner was a British subject. Today, the atmosphere is so richly evocative of plantation life in antebellum Louisiana that the house is much in demand as a film set. The haunting, Grand Guignol Bette Davis movie, *Hush...Hush Sweet Charlotte*, was made here in 1964.

Lyndhurst
Tarrytown, New York
1838–41; remodelled 1864–65

This country house commands a magnificent view from the east bank of the Hudson river and is now a favourite with visitors to the historic-house museums concentrated in this part of the Hudson valley. It was originally built as a weekend villa by a wealthy mayor of New York City, William Paulding, and his son, Philip R. Paulding. Their wish was for a house built in the then ultra-fashionable Gothic style and a leading architect of the genre, Alexander Jackson Davis (1803–92), was commissioned to furnish the design.

Davis found it frustrating that the Pauldings, like many rich clients of the time, failed to understand the importance of the architect being in charge, consequently, '... the mullions of the

Founder's Hall, Girard College,
Philadelphia, Pennsylvania.

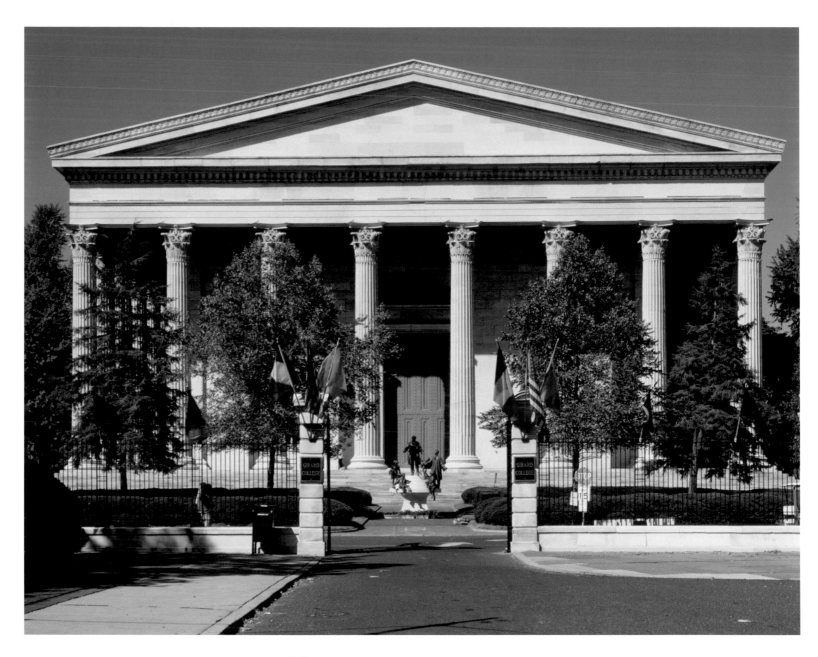

windows were made too small by nearly one half; the drip stones and copings incorrect and vulgar'. He got his chance to put things right in 1864, however, when the house's new owner, George Merritt, a wealthy merchant from Troy, New York, who had patented an innovative spring for a railroad car and was able to retire on the proceeds, asked Davis to return and enlarge the house.

By the time he had finished, Davis had nearly doubled the size of the house. He added a dining-room wing and other extensions to the ground plan is a series of steps back from the original facade and with lower rooflines, which helped to balance the additions with the original house, the whole structure was given the recesses and projections expected of a building in the Gothic style. His bold addition of a tower, 100ft (30m) high, resembling that of an English parish church, was the final perfect touch to this Gothic villa above the Hudson river.

Lyndhurst's most famous owner was the railroad baron, Jay Gould, who bought the house and 550 acres (220 hectares) of land in 1880 as a summer retreat for his family near New York City. Every day during the week, he would sail down the Hudson in his steam yacht, *Atalanta*, to his offices in New York, and at weekends would indulge his favourite pastimes of raising orchids and reading, while keeping an eye on the works in his art gallery, which George Merritt had converted from the Pauldings' original second-floor library.

When the last of Jay Gould's six children, Anna, dowager Duchesse de Tayleyrand-Périgord, died in France in 1961, she left Lyndhurst to its present owner, the National Trust for

Historic Preservation. Today the spectacular house, set in equally spectacular landscaped gardens, attracts thousands of visitors every summer.

Girard College
Philadelphia, Pennsylvania
1847

Stephen Girard was born in France in 1750 and arrived in Philadelphia in 1776. A banker in what was then America's most important business community, he became one of the wealthiest men in the country. He was the main inspiration behind the founding and building of Philadelphia's Merchants' Exchange (page 140), but perhaps his finest contribution to his adopted country was Girard College. In his will, he left money to endow a board school (referred to in his will as a 'college'), and when Girard College opened in January 1848 it was the world's first residential school for disadvantaged children.

No expense was spared in the building of what is today one of America's leading residential schools for 'academically capable pupils from families with limited financial resources' (to quote its website). The architect was Thomas Ustick Walter (1804–87), who had recently remodelled the galleries in Philadelphia's famous Christ Church, so that the church's beautiful Doric columns were relieved of the encumbering embrace of earlier galleries.

In his design for Girard College, Walter gave full reign to his love of the Greek Revival style, choosing to turn a pagan Greek temple into a place of academic learning. He designed the building, now called Founder's Hall, as a 'correct' replica

RIGHT, OPPOSITE: & PAGE 162: Trinity

Church, Boston, Massachusetts.

English Pre-Raphaelite artist, Edward Burne-Jones, and made in the William Morris Arts and Crafts studios in England in the 1880s. Frederick Clay Bartlett painted murals on the sanctuary walls depicting the Tree of Life from Genesis and Revelations, and a procession of angels with medieval musical instruments beneath a starry sky.

A recent addition is the church's Celtic Cross, made in 1957 on the Scottish island of Iona, home of Celtic Christianity. Noted for the quality of its metalwork, the cross is only the latest on a list of treasures that makes the Second Presbyterian Church one of Chicago's architectural highlights.

Trinity Church
Boston, Massachusetts
1872–77

Boston's Trinity Church, on Clarendon Street in stylish Back Bay, is a defining example of 'Richardsonian Romanesque', the unique and influential style of architecture perfected by Henry Hobson Richardson (1838–86) in the second half of the 19th century.

Richardson studied architecture at Harvard and, like so many of his contemporaries in America and England, at the influential École des Beaux-Arts in Paris. During his three years in Paris, from 1859 to 1862, he spent time in the studio of the architect Henri Labrouste, remembered today for his monumental libraries, in which steel frames were encased in masonry. Richardson's was a revival style, so typical of the 19th century, which in his case was based not on the architecture of Greece or Rome, but on the Romanesque

BELOW & OPPOSITE: Boston Public Library, Boston, Massachusetts.

Leon Battista Alberti. It presents a strong yet simple face to the world, with a triple-arched main entrance set centrally and with small, rectangular windows to either side. Above, at second-floor level, are larger, arched windows framed in sculptured stonework. In contrast, the library's inner atrium courtyard shows, above the ground-level cloisters, four ranges of windows rising to roof level.

The interior of the library is richly decorated. Both the entry hall and the main reading room have barrel-vaulted ceilings, while a richly carved limestone balcony, its back wall painted with murals depicting religious/historical scenes, looks down on the reading room. The library's superb murals, the theme of which is 'The Triumph of Religion', were the work of John Singer Sargent and the first were installed in the 'Hebraic' end of the library in 1895. The whole set took him 25 years to complete and they were not all finally installed until after his death in 1925.

Other artists whose work is in the Boston Public Library includes that of the painters Edwin Austin Abbey and Pierre Puvis de Chavannes, and of sculptors Bela Pratt, Augustus Saint-Gaudens and Daniel Chester French.

A Renaissance palazzo that was also an important milestone in the American late-19th-century architectural Renaissance, the recently restored Boston Public Library is also one of the great libraries of the world.

Banff Springs Hotel
Banff, Alberta, Canada
1888

The completion of the Canadian Pacific Railroad across Canada in 1885, not only connected both sides of the great country, it also revealed the glories of the Rockies to travellers from the east who would, of course, need somewhere to stay. William Cornelius Van Horne, president of the CPR, had long realized that in order to make the railroad pay, he would have to sell the Rockies as a superb scenic attraction to plenty of tourists. He responded to the problem in splendid style with what became a chain of hotels and alpine lodges that served hundreds of thousands of travellers to the western provinces of Canada.

OPPOSITE & LEFT: Grand Central
Terminal, Manhattan, New York.

Street, was designed initially by Reed & Stern, a Minnesota firm specializing in railroad design. When the Beaux-Arts-trained New York firm of Warren & Wetmore took over the project in 1911, however, conventional design went out of the window and New York got a 20th-century Roman basilica instead, built round a basic iron frame.

With the railroad tracks and their 100 or more platforms concealed on two levels underground – a scheme made possible by the fact that the station would be served only by electric trains – architectural attention could be trained on what was to be above the ground.

At the heart of the terminal was a spectacular main concourse that soon became famous, not only for the size of its meeting floor (it measures 120 x 375ft/37 x 114m), but for the glorious spaciousness of its design. Its vaulted ceiling, 125ft (38m) above the concourse floor, was painted by the French artist Paul Helleu, who used a zodiac design of 2,500 stars in the heavens, with lights pinpointing the major constellation, while light filters through three great 75-ft (23-m) arched windows on each side. The grand staircase, comprising two double flights of marble steps with brass handrails, was inspired by that of the Paris Opera House – and has, in turn, inspired many a scene in films and books.

Beyond the main concourse, Grand Central Station boasts a Vanderbilt Hall in Beaux-Arts style, complete with golden chandeliers and pink marble, and an enormous dining concourse, where the Grand Central Oyster Bar, with its yellow Gustavino tiles, has long been one of the most popular of the station's many places where meals are available.

OPPOSITE, LEFT & PAGE 180: Grand Central Terminal, Manhattan, New York.

That Grand Central still exists and has not gone the way of Pennsylvania Station, is due to a decision of the U.S. Supreme Court, which in 1978 declared it a historic landmark, thus saving it from demolition. It did not save it from being dwarfed by the rather ugly Met Life building, however, that rears up behind its colonnaded 42nd Street facade. But that is something of which the station's daily half-million commuters are unaware, once they are confronted with the magnificence inside.

Pennsylvania Station
Manhattan, New York, NY
1906–10

The railway age brought with it many new challenges for architects, particularly in America, where the railroad developed into one of the largest and most prestigious industries in the country. By the time the New York firm of McKim, Mead & White won the commission to build this latest New York terminal, it was well established as the country's leading exponent of the Neoclassical, Beaux-Arts-influenced style of urban architecture that had been challenging that of the Chicago School since the early 1890s. Even so, New York was astonished when it saw the result.

Certainly, it had the typical glass-and-metal shed leading to the trains, familiar to railroad passengers the world over. (Monet painted a brilliant series of trains waiting in the glass-covered sheds at Gare St.-Lazare in Paris in the 1870s, discharging their steam to mingle with the dappled light.) But in front of the shed at Pennsylvania Station was a concourse that was nothing less than breathtaking. Simple and functional but also sophisticated

and monumental in style, it was an almost exact copy of the tepidarium in the Baths of Caracalla in Rome. With its Corinthian columns, great arched windows and marble stairways, it was a monument to the railroads of America in the form of a Classical basilica.

Pennsylvania Station was demolished in 1963 and was replaced by a new terminal beneath the Madison Square Garden Center built on its site. Its demolition, which caused a great public outcry, concentrated the minds of New Yorkers on the need or otherwise to continually demolish and rebuild great swathes of the city, and two years after the station's demise, the New York City Landmarks Preservation Commission was established to secure the protection of New York's historic buildings and monuments. In 1974 the Commission's powers were extended to include the protection of historic interiors.

Many more New York buildings have been designated historic landmarks and have had preservation orders put on them in the past decades than might otherwise have been the case if the demolition of Pennsylvania Station, a wonderfully impressive entry to a great city, had not caused such a furore at the time.

U.S. Custom House (Alexander Hamilton Custom House: U.S. Bankruptcy Court)
Manhattan, New York, NY
1899–1907

Bowling Green goes back a long way in the history of New York, the Dutch having built a fort here, at the southern tip of Manhattan Island, to protect themselves from Native Americans

CHAPTER FOUR

NEW STRUCTURES & NEW MATERIALS
IN AN AGE OF ENTERPRISE c.1840–c.1900

The Balloon Frame

Haughwout Building, New York, NY

Brooklyn Bridge, New York, NY

'Painted Ladies' (Victorians), San Francisco, California

Rookery Building, Chicago, Illinois

Wainwright Building, St. Louis, Missouri

Carson Pirie Scott Store, Chicago, Illinois

OPPOSITE & LEFT: Views of the
Brooklyn Bridge, New York City.

OPPOSITE & LEFT: Views of the
Brooklyn Bridge, New York City.

bedevilled by budget overruns and the deaths of 20 workers, most of them from caisson disease (the 'bends') after returning to the surface from the underwater excavation chambers.

Before he had even begun work on the foundations for the bridge's piers, however, Roebling was seriously injured when his foot was crushed between a slipway and a ferry: tetanus set in and he died of his injuries three weeks later. His eldest son, Washington August Roebling (1837–1926) took over as chief engineer and saw the project through, despite being virtually confined to his home after 1872, when he was partially paralysed and deafened – stricken with the bends after working all day installing one of the bridge's pneumatic caissons, which were in water up to 78ft (24m) deep.

The Roeblings' bridge had a central span of 1,604ft (489m). It was supported by four steel cables, fastened to a series of anchor bars held in place by cast-iron anchor plates, and an intricate web of radiating stays and suspender wires on two 297-ft (90-m) granite towers. The towers, rising from caissons each the size of four tennis courts, incorporated Gothic peaked arches and were modelled on the skyscrapers that were then springing up in New York. The bridge, which was given a floor resting on 4-ton steel beams, was made wide enough to have two outer lanes for carriages, two lines for cable cars, and an elevated centre walkway.

Brooklyn Bridge, given its miraculous marriage of function and form, impressed not only architects, engineers and technologists, it also made an extraordinary impression on artists and writers. Henry Miller, for instance, felt that 'The bridge was the harp of death, the strange winged creature without an eye which held me suspended between the two shores'.

Of course, there is no need to remain suspended between the two shores: it takes about 20 minutes to walk across the bridge to Brooklyn from the beginning of the pedestrian walkway just east of City Hall. The walk usually takes longer, however, because there are observation points under both stone support towers, with histories of the waterfront that tend to slow walkers up.

'Painted Ladies' (Victorians)
San Francisco, California
From c.1860s

The balloon frame came to San Francisco with the great California Gold Rush of 1848 – not that too many San Franciscans recognized their future dwellings in the cheap, partially prefabricated houses and iron sheds rushed from the east to accommodate the more than 25,000 diggers who flocked to the area in the year following the first discoveries.

As in Chicago, so in San Francisco, and the rapid growth of the village into a thriving – and often lawless – town was made bearable for its inhabitants by the speed with which new houses could be thrown up. As time passed, San Francisco's better-off citizens, many of them made wealthy by the rich and dependable silver Comstock Lode, took their scruffy town in hand and gave it wide avenues, parks, a system of cable cars, and better housing.

They also took the basic balloon frame and embellished it, and whole neighbourhoods of these houses, which came to be called 'Victorians', because they took their styles and embellishments from Victorian England, sprang up in the city.

OPPOSITE: The East River at night, with the Brooklyn and Manhattan Bridges.

Victorian houses in Alamo Square, San Francisco, California.

The grandest of them all were clustered around Pacific Heights and Nob Hill, but there were many in other districts, including the Western Addition, the outer Mission and the Haight, most of which were built of redwood from the Marin Headlands across the Golden Gate.

To the basic, simple clapboard balloon frame was added an array of balconies, bay windows and towers in a wonderfully exuberant range of styles, including Gothic, French château, Italian, English Queen Anne (early Georgian) and even Turkish (usually in the form of minaret-like towers). Many of the large, grand houses of San Francisco's rich were built of stone or brick and covered in stucco, and were given heavy cornices and quantities of moulded decorative stonework around windows. Neighbours vied with one another in the wealth of 'signature details' they could add to their houses' already ornate facades.

Many of San Francisco's splendid Victorians disappeared in the earthquake of 1906 and the fire that followed. When the parts of San Francisco that had known the quirkiest balloon-framed Victorians became the centre of the 1960s hippie scene, the Victorians that remained – some 13,000 of them – were rediscovered. Rescue and renovation followed, much of which involved painting the houses in rainbow colours, sometimes with four or more colours on a single house – a fashion which earned San Francisco's Victorians their popular name, 'Painted Ladies'.

At first slow, renovation was subsequently rapid and expensive once the dot.com boom hit San Francisco. Although that particular bubble subsequently burst, the market for 'saved' Victorians remains strong – much to the relief of the city's many speculators in real estate.

Alamo Square and the San Francisco skyline beyond.

RIGHT & FAR RIGHT: Burnham & Root's
Rookery Building, Chicago, Illinois.

OPPOSITE & PAGE 204: The Rookery
Building's interior lobby atrium was
remodelled by Frank Lloyd Wright in
1905–07.

**Rookery Building
Chicago, Illinois
1885–88**

After the great Chicago Fire of 1871, a temporary city hall and
large water tower were erected on LaSalle Street, the tower
becoming a favourite roosting place for the city's pigeon

population until it was pulled down. This accounts for the unlikely name of the Rookery Building, built on the same site and designed by the Chicago architectural partnership of Daniel Hudson Burnham (1846–1912) and John Wellborn Root (c.1850–91).

The style of the Burnham & Root partnership, one of the seminal collaborations belonging to the Chicago School of skyscraper design, owes much to Henry Hobson Richardson, whose highly individual buildings, all of them load-bearing constructions, display the same simple monumentality. This influence is particularly strong in the Rookery Building, an early work in the Burnham & Root repertoire.

Transitional in the evolution of the multi-storey building, that recent inventions and technical innovations had made possible, the Rookery combined a skeletal frame of iron and steel, its outer walls supported by masonry piers. Its design, largely the work of Daniel Burnham, was in the quasi-Romanesque style of Richardson's Marshall Field Warehouse in Chicago, its great mass softened by exterior ornamentatation in several styles by John Root, who was also responsible for the building's grillage foundation.

Burnham and Root gave the Rookery Building a lobby court at the foot of a spectacular interior atrium, designed to provide light for all the offices that did not face the street. But the lacy ironwork skylight, though delightfully airy, was not waterproof, and in 1905–07 the lobby atrium was remodelled by Frank Lloyd Wright. He retained the elegant ironwork, but filled it in with glass and also introduced elements characteristic of his Prairie House designs.

Designated a Chicago Landmark in 1972, and with its spectacular atrium restored in 1992, the Rookery Building is a high point on Chicago's long list of 'must-see' buildings, even though the pigeons have long since gone.

Wainwright Building
St. Louis, Missouri
1890–91

The ten-storey, all-steel-framed building that Louis Henri Sullivan (1856–1924) designed in partnership with Dankmar Adler (1844–1900) for Ellis Wainwright, a wealthy St. Louis brewer, was one of the Chicago architect's earliest attempts at a true multi-storeyed construction. Other architects of the day were also rising to the challenge and had been facing similar design problems, since recent advances in steel production had made such buildings possible; but it was the refinements that Sullivan was to bring to the technique of tall buildings, allied with his development of an organic theory of architecture, that made him the most influential architect of his day in America.

The Wainwright Building is architecturally significant because it demonstrates an early stage in the development of Sullivan's style in a way that Sullivan & Adler's earlier Auditorium Building in Chicago (page 221 et seq.) did not. At the time, many architects, in an attempt to incorporate old and familiar designs into multi-storey buildings, either simply repeated the same ornamentation, window shape and the like, from floor to floor up the building, or used the unifying arches of the Richardson Romanesque style up the height of the building, rather than crossing it horizontally.

OPPOSITE & LEFT: The Wainwright
Building, St. Louis, Missouri.

BELOW: The Wainwright Building, St. Louis, Missouri (detail).

OPPOSITE: Carson Pirie Scott Store, Chicago, Illinois.

Sullivan treated the Wainwright Building, a steel-framed construction clad in masonry, as if it were a column rather than a box. The two lower floors, unadorned except for their large, deep windows, provided the column's base, the remaining floors its shaft, and the ornately decorated frieze and cornice its capital.

Sullivan brought a sense of visual unity to the facades of the Wainwright Building by treating them as grids of horizontals and verticals. To emphasize the verticals, he broadened the building's corner piers and extended them, uninterrupted, to the cornice, while thinner piers between the windows also rose from the building's base to the cornice. The wealth of decorative features, including ornamental spandrels inserted between the piers, helped to tie the whole structure convincingly together.

The Wainwright Building fell into disrepair during St. Louis's mid-20th-century economic depression and came very near to demolition. The National Trust for Historic Preservation saved it by taking an option on the building, which was eventually acquired by the state of Missouri: it is now a distinguished element in a complex of state offices.

Carson Pirie Scott Store
Chicago, Illinois
1898–1904

One of Chicago's great department stores, Carson Pirie Scott was originally the Schlesinger-Mayer Store, named after the two businessmen who commissioned it from Louis Sullivan. It was one of Sullivan's last major commercial buildings, and is considered not only to be one of his best, but also one of the most important survivals from the early years of modern architecture.

Despite its corner site with a tower, added to Sullivan's original design at the insistence of the owners, the 12-storey Carson Pirie Scott Store follows the theory that tall buildings should be designed as columns – with a base, central shaft and capital – as Sullivan outlined in his essay 'The Tall Office Building Artistically Considered', and which he had already applied to his design for the Wainwright Building of 1890–91.

In contrast with the Wainwright Building, much of the intricate ornamentation on the Carson Pirie Scott Store,

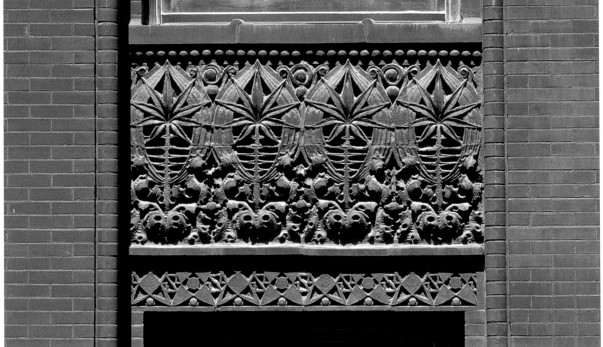

designed by Sullivan and made of cast iron clad with terracotta (unglazed fired clay), is carried on the two storeys forming the base of his column. The fluidity of the Art Nouveau-style design that frames the store's windows, allied with the solidity of the cast iron, lends a wonderful sense of animation, and is a fine example of Sullivan's genius in the field of architectural ornamentation. Above the base, the Carson Pirie Scott building's all-steel frame allows for grid-like facades, the spaces in between the grids' horizontals and verticals being filled with large 'picture' windows, so that the maximum amount of light can be admitted to the interior.

When it opened, the store's sales levels housed an art gallery, café, restaurant and an elegantly furnished lounge. This was in keeping with the practice, then common in Chicago and executed with considerable aplomb at Marshall Field's, a couple of blocks north on State Street, of making shopping a memorable experience.

A 12-storey addition to the south of Sullivan's building, and following its roofline, was added by Burnham and Root in 1905–06, with a third addition following in 1960–61. The store was designated a Chicago Landmark in 1970 and remains a consumer's paradise and one of Chicago's most architecturally important buildings.

THE RISE OF THE SKYSCRAPER
c.1870–c.1916

Leiter I Building (1879) and Leiter II Building (1889–91), Chicago, Illinois

Auditorium Building, Chicago, Illinois

Tacoma Building, Chicago, Illinois

Monadnock Building, Chicago, Illinois

Reliance Building, Chicago, Illinois

Guaranty Building, Buffalo, New York

Columbia University, New York

Flatiron Building, New York, NY

Sante Fe Building, Chicago, Illinois

David B. Gamble House, Pasadena, California

Woolworth Building, New York, NY

Equitable Building, New York, NY

CHAPTER FIVE
THE RISE OF THE SKYSCRAPER
c.1870–c.1916

RIGHT: Leiter II Building, Chicago, Illinois (1889–91). Architect: William Le Baron Jenney. (See page 217 et seq.)

OPPOSITE: Woolworth Building, Manhattan, New York (1911–13). Architect: Cass Gilbert. (See page 248 et seq.)

The fire that razed much of Chicago to the ground in 1871 proved to be a turning point for architecture in North America and, in the 20th century, in the rest of the world. The city, a gateway to the western prairies and a major rail and cattle depot, had been growing rapidly in the 19th century, and its future depended on it being rebuilt as quickly as possible. Entrepreneurs and architects alike took up the challenge with enthusiasm, but because building land in the city centre had been rocketing in price, commercial buildings had to be built tall, so that their promoters could recoup in rents what they had disbursed in land and building costs. They also had to be fireproof and durable.

The 'Chicago School' of architecture grew out of the great Chicago building boom, when a handful of architectural practices in the city, supported by promoters and businessmen full of confidence and enthusiasm, developed a style of metal-framed, multi-storey building that led to the first skyscrapers and, ultimately, to the architecturally simplified architecture of the 20th century. Buildings in the style of the Chicago School came to be constructed in many cities of the Midwest, especially in areas of warehousing and commercial use, and a large complex of such buildings appeared in Winnipeg, Canada.

The entrepreneurial and inventive skills of the age helped

212

architects to build tall. Ways of fire-proofing iron and steel girders were developed, the steam- or gas-driven elevator gave way to the hydraulic lift, and telephone and electric light systems became widespread.

In the buildings of the architects of the Chicago School, ornament tended to be subordinate to the structure, and if ornamentation was used, it was more often than not in the form of panels between windows and beneath pediments or on pilasters and columns. Terracotta (unglazed fired clay) was often used in ornamentation, and some buildings were entirely clad in the material.

The design style of the Chicago School, even in its heyday in the 1880s and 1890s, did not have everything its own way, as the World's Columbian Exposition of 1893 was to demonstrate. This six-month-long event, to which 46 nations were invited to submit a total of 250,000 exhibits and displays, was largely the project of Chicago architect, Daniel Burnham. He enlisted the famous garden architect, Frederick Law Olmsted, to plan a park-like setting for the fair, and called on many of America's leading architects to design the buildings. The result was a 'White City' of buildings designed mostly in the serenely Classical Greek Revival style, complete with white-columned porticoes and great domes.

Many architectural historians consider the World's Columbian Exposition to have been a retrograde step as far as architecture in America was concerned, due to the pernicious influence of those derivative Greek and Roman temples, no doubt. While it is true that a new wave of Classicism was spawning many massive and monumental structures in Chicago in the years before 1914, and the Classical influence was still

Leiter I and Leiter II Buildings
Chicago, Illinois
1879 and 1889–91

The two Leiter Buildings were the work of William Le Baron Jenney (1832–1907). Like many of his American contemporaries, Jenney studied in Paris, but while some of the finest American architects of the age learned their craft at the École des Beaux-Arts, Jenney attended the École Centrale des Arts et Manufactures. Perhaps as a result of this, his interest lay more in the technicalities of architecture than its aesthetics, leading him to concentrate more on a building's construction than its decoration.

Jenney ensured his place in the history of American architecture by being the first to use a frame, wholly made of steel, in a large or multi-storey building. The most famous of

this type was the Home Insurance Building (Chicago, 1883–85; demolished 1931), though he had incorporated steel frames into buildings before this time. His Ludington Building of 1881, to which he added a complete terracotta cladding, was built by Mary Ludington to house the American Book Company. It is the oldest steel-framed building still surviving in Chicago, and was designated a Chicago Landmark in 1996.

OPPOSITE & ABOVE: Leiter II Building, Chicago, Illinois.

FAR LEFT: Leiter I Building, Chicago, Illinois.

OPPOSITE: Leiter I Building, Chicago, Illinois (demolished 1972).

LEFT: The Auditorium Building, Chicago, Illinois.

was built on State Street in 1891 and was later leased by Sears, Roebuck and Company as its flagship Chicago store. Thus it can be seen as seminal in making State Street the important retail thoroughfare it is today. Leiter II is the city's oldest surviving department store and one of America's most significant early examples of skeleton-framed commercial architecture. It was designated a Chicago Landmark in 1997.

Auditorium Building
Chicago, Illinois
1886–90

This is another of Chicago's historic buildings to which words like 'turning point' and 'milestone' can equally be applied. The Auditorium Building was built during a decade of boom years for Chicago, a time when people were coming from all over the world, merely for a glimpse of what the future held in store. In 1880, only buildings of five or six storeys could be seen in the Loop, but by 1890 the steel frame had made much taller buildings possible, and William Le Baron Jenney's steel-framed Manhattan Building (1890) could claim the distinction of being the first 16-storey building in America.

As is the case in a flourishing economy the world over, Chicago's civic amenities were neglected in the rush to profit from the commercial and industrial prosperity that beckoned, and names like 'Porkopolis' were soon given to Chicago by older cities back East. The Auditorium Building, financed by a group of local civic leaders, was built to counteract the impression that greed was paramount and create a climate in which high culture would flourish in Chicago.

A leading architectural practice of the day, Adler & Sullivan, was commissioned to design Chicago's new cultural centre. The brilliant engineering talent of Dankmar Adler (1844–1900) and the architectural genius of Louis Henri Sullivan (1856–1924) combined to create a huge ten-storey block on Michigan Avenue, with an additional ten-storey tower 'weighing 30 million pounds' (according to Sullivan) on top. The building housed a theatre large enough to stage grand opera for an audience of over 4,000, a hotel and an office building. Sullivan described the Auditorium Building in his *The Autobiography of an Idea*, published in 1924, as 'a tower of solid masonry carried on a "floating foundation"; a great raft 67 by 100 feet'.

Sullivan designed the exterior of the building in a relatively restrained style. It was a solidly built, almost fortress-like two-stage rectangular structure, with arched windows and fluted columns designed in a simplified Richardsonian Romanesque style: Sullivan was not yet articulating the exteriors of his buildings in a way that expressed their internal structure.

There was nothing restrained about the interior, however, which Sullivan decorated in lavish style. He made great use of gold in the murals and mosaics that decorated the walls, applied gold leaf to the plaster reliefs that adorned the hotel lobby, bar, dining room and theatre, and installed hundreds of the new electric light bulbs to illuminate the whole. The interior of the theatre was the grandest of all, with its four elliptical arches emphasizing the proscenium and more lavishly decorated arches that framed murals around the walls.

The Auditorium Building, which was designated a Chicago

OPPOSITE & FAR LEFT: The Auditorium Building, Chicago, Illinois.

Landmark in 1976, has been owned by Roosevelt University since 1946. The university houses its library in the former hotel dining room, but the Auditorium Theatre remains one of Chicago's leading theatrical and musical venues, and one of American architecture's most original buildings.

Tacoma Building
Chicago, Illinois
1889

Born in New York, and a military cadet at West Point for two years, William Holabird (1854–1923) chose to move to Chicago in 1875 to pursue a career in architecture. He joined the architectural practice of William Le Baron Jenney, then deeply immersed in planning iron- and steel-framed buildings for the rapidly growing post-fire city. After five years with Jenney, Holabird established his own practice in 1880, and the next year formed a partnership with another of Jenney's architects, Martin Roche (1855–1927), who had been raised in Chicago and educated at the Armour Institute of Technology (now ITT). The architectural practice of Holabird & Roche was to become one of the most prolific in Chicago and a distinguished part of the Chicago School.

The Tacoma Building, in Chicago's Loop, was one of the new partnership's earliest designs. It was a 13-storey, steel-framed building, with a store and entrance lobby on the ground floor and offices above. The facade, virtually devoid of ornamentation, made extensive use of glass, and had the projecting bays rising from above the ground floor to the top of the building that were to become a feature of Chicago School design. The windows were also designed in the distinctive 'Chicago window' style, in which a large central pane of glass was flanked by narrow sash windows that could be opened.

By 1905, when their Chicago Building on Madison Street was completed, Holabird and Roche had virtually perfected their contribution to the by now internationally recognized Chicago School, adding terracotta cladding to the typical mix of metal-frame construction, distinctive projecting bays and Chicago windows.

The Chicago Building, designated a Chicago Landmark in 1996, still stands proudly among the architecturally significant buildings that cluster about the corner of Madison and State, once 'the world's busiest corner'. The Tacoma Building was not so lucky, however. It had not been dubbed a Chicago Landmark and was demolished in 1993.

Holabird and Roche continued to be a force in Chicago architecture well into the 20th century. Two years after Martin Roche died, William Holabird's son, John A. Holabird (1886–1963) reorganized his father's firm by going into partnership with another son of a famous Chicago architect. This was John Wellborn Root Jr., son of the great Daniel Burnham's first partner. Holabird & Root's great Art Deco skyscraper, the Chicago Board of Trade Building (1930), was given its Chicago Landmark designation in 1977.

Monadnock Building
Chicago, Illinois
1889–91; 1891–93

This building, situated on West Jackson Boulevard, was built in two halves, the northern half by the influential design team of

OPPOSITE: The Auditorium Building, Chicago, Illinois.

THIS PAGE & OPPOSITE: The

Monadnock Building, Chicago, Illinois.

Daniel Hudson Burnham (1846–1912) and John Wellborn Root (1850–91) in 1889–91, and the southern addition by another leading Chicago practice, Holabird & Roche, in 1891–93. Together, the two parts of the Monadnock Building offer a unique perspective into the development of the tall building in Chicago.

The northern half is a powerful, sparsely ornamented 16-storey building on West Jackson Street. It was the last Chicago skyscraper to be constructed with load-bearing walls, with brick the chosen material. According to Louis Sullivan, writing in *The Autobiography of an Idea* (New York, 1924), Burnham and Root prepared plans for the Monadnock Building but, because they would be making a big jump from the nine storeys then more usual in load-bearing buildings in Chicago, delayed construction 'until it should be seen whether or not the Auditorium Tower would go to China of its own free will…'. Once it was seen not to be collapsing beneath its own weight, work began on the Monadnock Building.

Sullivan may have been correct in giving this reason for the delay, but it was perhaps the client rather than Burnham and Root who was apprehensive about its height, for the architects had planned their building carefully, giving it walls 6ft (1.8m) thick at the base, which thinned out as the building rose.

Sullivan's description of the building cannot be bettered: '…an amazing cliff of brickwork, rising sheer and stark, with a subtlety of line and surface, a direct singleness of purpose, that gave one the thrill of romance.' Much of that subtlety of line and surface came from the way in which Burnham and Root gently modulated the building's profile. The oriel-style window bays,

filled with narrow vertical windows, projected only moderately, and rose from above the base of the building all the way to the top, each in one elegant line.

Holabird & Roche's southern addition was an early example of a steel-frame construction, the underlying bones of which were clearly visible through the facade's narrow piers and wide windows.

The Monadnock Building, still the world's tallest all-masonry structure, was designated a Chicago Landmark in 1973.

Reliance Building
Chicago, Illinois
1890, 1894–95

This spectacular construction on State Street, designed by Burnham & Root, is very different from the load-bearing Monadnock Building, which was still being completed when work began on the base of the Reliance Building. For a start, it has a steel frame, with a pronounced verticality of line. Then, there is all that glass! To startled Chicagoans of the 1890s, the Reliance Building's glass-covered exterior seemed to defy gravity. To the architectural historians of today, however, it is, quite simply, the direct ancestor of the metal-and-glass skyscrapers of the later 20th century.

The two-storey base was constructed in 1890 and its 12 upper floors in 1894–95. Burnham & Root gave the upper floors very narrow piers, mullions and spandrels, and covered them in cream-coloured terracotta, decorated with Gothic-style tracery. This made a light, almost delicate-looking web in which to set the building's windows, some of them set flat into the facade, others

Reliance Building, Chicago, Illinois.

RIGHT & OPPOSITE: Reliance Building,
Chicago, Illinois.

in projecting bays. The style of the windows – a wide, fixed pane flanked by narrow sash windows – came to be known as the 'Chicago window'. As in their Monadnock Building, the projecting window bays in Burnham & Root's Reliance Building rose from the base up the full height of the building to its flat cornice, adding to its strongly vertical line.

Once one of the most elegant in Chicago, the Reliance Building was allowed to fall into disrepair in the later 20th century. The City of Chicago bought it in 1994, designated it a Chicago Landmark in 1995 (it is also listed as a National Historic Landmark) and completely restored it, discovering the lovely creamy-white terracotta that had been such a feature of the exterior beneath years of grime. In 1999 the Reliance Building reopened to the world as a fine hotel, with 103 rooms and 19 elegant suites. It is now named the Hotel Burnham after its designer, Daniel Burnham.

Guaranty Building
Buffalo, New York
1894–95

Louis Sullivan's Buffalo office block, the deep-red terracotta Guaranty Building, and his 1899 Carson Pirie Scott Store in Chicago (page 208), are the buildings that, for architectural historians, mark the point at which the building of a skyscraper ceased to be a scientific and engineering exercise and became an instinctive art.

During the 1890s Sullivan concentrated almost exclusively on designing skyscraper offices for a large client list in Chicago and several other cities. A single theme underlay the design of

Guaranty Building, Buffalo, New York.

Guaranty Building, Buffalo, New York.
Exterior detail.

THIS PAGE & OPPOSITE: Views of the Flatiron Building, Manhattan, New York.

for the design. The firm gave the university a campus that was a model of architectural Classicism, as though ignorant of the fact that a quite different architectural style had been at work in Chicago, and even New York, for nearly two decades.

Columbia's first new buildings were set around a central quadrangle, dominated by the Low Library (1895–97), a building with an imposing Greek Revival facade, with a Corinthian-columned central portico and a great dome set centrally above. In 1903 an imposing statue, *Alma Mater*, by Daniel Chester French, was set up on the wide flight of marble steps leading to the library's main entrance. The statue survived a bomb blast in 1968, when the university's students, clearly a lot more rebellious than the class of 1897, demonstrated in protest at the university's plans to build a gymnasium in nearby Morningside Park.

McKim, Mead & White continued to design buildings in Classical style for Columbia University well into the 20th century. Particularly notable was the School of Journalism (1912), founded by Joseph Pulitzer and home today of the Pulitzer Prize, awarded for outstanding contributions to music and letters.

Flatiron Building
Manhattan, New York, NY
1902

More properly called the Fuller Building, after the construction company that commissioned Daniel Burnham to build it, the Flatiron Building on Fifth Avenue was given other names during its construction, including 'Burnham's Folly'.

RIGHT: Flatiron Building, Manhattan, New York.

OPPOSITE: Santa Fe Building, Chicago, Illinois.

But it was not long before New Yorkers decided that, because of its extraordinary triangular shape, the name Flatiron was more appropriate. So it has remained and has even given its name to the Flatiron District, an up-and-coming shopping area of New York.

One of the earliest steel-framed constructions in New York, the 20-storey Flatiron Building was the tallest in the world when it was completed in 1902. Its shape was dictated by the way in which Daniel Burnham chose to make the best use of a site made triangular by the meeting of Fifth Avenue, Broadway and 23rd Street. The tag Burnham's Folly arose because many feared that winds created by the building's shape and height (it was 300ft/91m) high) could well blow it down or that it would simply collapse beneath its own weight.

The Flatiron did not collapse, of course, neither did it blow down – though the undeniable wind that blows along 23rd Street did cause skirts to lift and men to hope for a glimpse of a well-turned female ankle. Nor was the Flatiron the 'tallest building' for long: within five years of its completion, the New York skyline was being radically altered by buildings topping 500ft (150m) or more.

The influence of Louis Sullivan and the Chicago School was more than apparent in Burnham's design for the Flatiron Building. Here was Sullivan's ideal tall office block, designed along the lines of a Classical column, with a base housing shops and a lobby, a middle section with as many office floors as the client desired, and a top, or attic, floor. Here also were the arches over the top rows of windows and the lines of gently protruding window bays rising at intervals along the facades

that were familiar features in the skyscrapers of Chicago. The Flatiron's ornamentation was designed by Frederick P. Dinkelberg, who was also responsible for the decoration of Burnham's Railway Exchange Building (now the Santa Fe Building, below) and the Heyworth Building in Chicago.

Santa Fe Building
Chicago, Illinois
1904

Designed by Daniel Burnham in the typical style of the Chicago School and given an arresting creamy-white terracotta facade, this 17-storey construction opened as the Railway Exchange Building in 1904. In its early years its importance lay in the fact that Daniel Burnham had his office on the 14th floor, during the time he was working on his Plan of Chicago of 1909.

This great plan for the regeneration of Chicago grew out of the World's Columbian Exposition (also known as the Chicago World's Fair) of 1893. Many of America's leading architects of the day designed buildings for the exposition's White City, with Charles B. Atwood of the D.H. Burnham Company contributing an amazing Classical Greek temple for the Palace of Fine Arts (rebuilt in permanent form in the 1920s). The harmonious, serenely elegant Classical architecture, and the careful planning of the exposition, stood in sharp contrast to the black industrial city of Chicago that lay to the north. It demonstrated to Chicagoans how their city might be transformed from a grimy place of business to a 'city beautyful' and gave Daniel Burnham the impetus to do something about the state of his home city.

Santa Fe Building, Chicago, Illinois.

Realizing his Plan of Chicago was going to be big, Daniel Burnham built a penthouse on the north-east corner of the top of the Santa Fe Building. Here the plans were prepared and here visitors were able to see the work in progress. The plan resulted in the completion of a series of major public works in Chicago in the decades that followed.

In the 1980s the light well that Daniel Burnham had introduced through the centre of the building was closed using a large skylight. Today, renamed the Santa Fe Building, Burnham's gleaming white office block is home to the Chicago Architectural Foundation and to the Chicago office of the internationally-renowned architectural practice of Skidmore, Owings & Merrill, among others.

David B. Gamble House
Pasadena, California
1908–09

While craftsman furniture-maker Gustav Stickley ensured the popularity of the Arts and Crafts bungalow across America, it was the architect brothers Charles Sumner Greene (1868–1957) and Henry Mather Greene (1870–1954) who took the bungalow in California to an unprecedented level of architectural design

BELOW, PAGES 244 & 245: Gamble House, Pasadena, California.

and craftmanship. Among the houses in the 'Shingle Style' they built for wealthy Californians, the house in Pasadena, intended as a winter residence for David B. Gamble and his wife of Cincinnati, Ohio, remains a truly outstanding example of a Craftsman-style single-storey house.

The Gambles were wealthy: David Gamble was a second-generation member of the Proctor & Gamble family and the couple decided, after ten years of spending their winters in resort hotels in Pasadena, to build a house of their own instead. Adjoining the building lot they bought for the purpose was

another property on which a new house was being built. They liked the look of it, talked to its architects, and commissioned a similar house from themselves.

The architects were the Greene brothers and, like the Gambles, originally hailed from Cincinnati, but had spent part of their childhood on a family farm in West Virginia. Here, they had developed a love of nature that remained with them throughout their years of education, having studied woodworking, metalwork and toolmaking at the Manual Training School of Washington University, and the traditional classic building styles at the Massachusetts Institute of Technology's School of Architecture. Their parents had already moved to the 'little country town' of Pasadena in California and in 1893 the brothers decided to join them. On their way, they stopped in Chicago and visited the World's Columbian Exposition, where they encountered Japanese design and architecture for the first time.

As American architects, and as a result of these influences, the Greene brothers came closest to achieving the Craftsman ideal. They chose to work only in wood and their design styles and building methods grew directly from their intimate knowledge of the material. Their buildings' surfaces were opened up by the lines and angles of the projections and recesses given them by the Greenes. A Greene and Greene house was always set in natural garden surroundings, but plantings was kept at arm's length and climbing plants were not allowed to obscure the buildings' lines.

The house that Greene and Greene built for the Gambles, and the furnishings they designed for it, were masterpieces of

the Craftsman style. The low-eaved exterior – in part inspired by the Japanese exhibits the Greenes had seen in Chicago – was built of California redwood, gently rounded and polished to encourage the play of light on the wood, while the magnificence of the redwood, teak and mahogany used in the interior was enhanced by the subtle light that filtered through stained-glass windows and doors. Everything, from the beams of the supporting structure to the frames around the doors, were carefully jointed and meticulously finished.

The house remained in the Gamble family until 1966, when ownership was transferred to the city of Pasadena in a joint agreement with the University of Southern California School of Architecture. Today, the Gamble House on Westmoreland Place is the only example of the Greene and Greene style to have survived with its original, flawlessly-designed Greene and Greene furniture and furnishings intact.

Woolworth Building
Manhattan, New York, NY
1911–13

There are gargoyle-like bas-relief caricatures of its architect, Cass Gilbert (1859–1934), and its owner, Frank Winfield Woolworth, in the lobby of the Woolworth Building at 233 Broadway. This is entirely appropriate since the marble-walled, glass mosaic-domed lobby itself evokes the interior of a great Gothic church. Its central axis suggests a church's nave, and the smaller lobbies housing the elevators are reminiscent of side chapels. With its wealth of golden filigree tracery, painted decoration and sculptured reliefs, the lobby of the Woolworth Building is one of the City of New York's great architectural treasures.

As is the building for which the lobby was designed: the Woolworth Building was constructed as the headquarters of the international chain of variety stores founded by Frank Woolworth, who was a simple salesman when he opened his first store in 1879, in which low-priced goods were sold. Now, in 1913, he was one of the richest men in America and had as his headquarters – for which he paid $13.5 million in cash, though not perhaps in nickels and dimes, as was rumoured at the time – a true 'Cathedral of Commerce', as it was dubbed by a local clergyman.

Following Frank Woolworth's expressed wish for a building that echoed the Houses of Parliament in London, which he greatly admired, Cass Gilbert provided a style that was both picturesque and consciously evocative of the great buildings of medieval Europe, its vertical lines, with pinnacles over the ranges of windows at several levels, recalling those of a Gothic cathedral. The multi-storeyed tower that topped the building came complete with a handsomely decorated spire, the Gothic detailing on which was deliberately made oversized, so that it could be seen from a considerable distance away. Gilbert added to the building's soaring lines by increasing the distance between floors, thus making space for taller windows. This also meant, however, that the Woolworth Building was able to accommodate only 58 floors in the 792ft (241m) available, whereas a present-day, rent-conscious designer would cram 80 floors into such a height.

The Woolworth Building was officially opened on 24 April 1913, when President Theodore Roosevelt pressed a button in the

The Woolworth Building, Manhattan, New York.

RIGHT: The Woolworth Building, Manhattan, New York.

OPPOSITE: The Equitable Building, under construction in Manhattan, New York.

White House to illuminate it inside and out. It was an appropriately imaginative opening ceremony for what was then the tallest building in the city, and it did not lose this title until 1930, when the Chrysler Building was built. Technically advanced in its construction, the Woolworth Building was also so stylish that it remained an exemplar of skyscraper design in New York into the 1920s and early 1930s.

Gilbert's greatest technological innovation in the Woolworth Building lay in its foundations. When it was finished, it was the tallest building ever constructed without a bedrock foundation. Gilbert countered the load of the building by sinking a series of caissons 110ft (33m) into the soil, in much the same way as bridges are built.

The Woolworth Building was designated a New York Historic Landmark in 1983. The great building is now owned by the Witkoff Group, which bought it for $155 million in 1998. Its remarkable lobby, and a museum room containing the Empire-style furnishings from Frank Woolworth's private office, are open to the public in office hours. Otherwise, the Woolworth Building is still very much a cathedral of commerce.

Equitable Building
Manhattan, New York, NY
1915

The most important thing about this Beaux-Arts-style limestone-clad skyscraper, built for the Equitable Life Insurance Company in 1915, was not its height, although its 41 storeys put it among the taller buildings in New York. It was in fact a problem, which was its shape: the building rose straight up with no setbacks, consequently, buildings in the vicinity were deprived of natural light.

For years, New York and Chicago had been competitors in the business of building ever taller buildings at greater and greater speed. They were both fast-growing cities, where the value of available land was rising as rapidly as it was being used up, and to make money, builders needed to maximize the usable and rentable space that could be obtained from every lot. As early as 1898, by which time the streets of New York were growing darker and darker, Ernest Flagg, architect of the Singer Building (1906–08) had suggested that only the base of any new building should be allowed to extend as far as the street, with projecting towers restricted to a quarter of the site's size.

The Equitable Building's architects, Ernest R. Graham & Associates (later Graham, Anderson, Probst & White) designed a building of 'glorious and immense volume'. It had 1,206,500sq ft (112000m²) of floor area on a plot just under an acre in size, or floor space almost 30 times the area of the site. Such exploitation of a site was unprecedented and caused a great furore, forcing New York's city fathers to take action.

The result was America's first comprehensive zoning resolution, passed in 1916, which adopted Ernest Flagg's suggestion of nearly 20 years earlier. From then on, New York's skyscrapers had to be built back from the street, a ruling that resulted in a great, and not always happy, change in skyscraper style. Too many buildings in the next decades were built in badly proportioned tiers, 'like wedding cakes', as was remarked by a disapproving critic.

CHAPTER SIX

EUROPEAN MODERNISM
& THE AMERICAN SPIRIT
1900–c.1960

EUROPEAN MODERNISM
& THE AMERICAN SPIRIT
1900–c.1960

A merica carried into the 20th century the go-ahead, exuberantly optimistic approach to architecture that had characterized its buildings in the late 19th century. Nowhere was this more obvious than in Florida. Here, one of the great fortunes made from oil had funded the extension of the railroad network into the heart of the state in the 1890s, and set it on its way to becoming the great winter playground of the wealthy in the United States.

Florida's entrepreneurs were quick to recognize the opportunities for development now on offer, with the result that building flourished. The wealthy not only built large, architect-designed holiday homes for themselves, but also whole towns and suburbs of towns to house more ordinary visitors. Largely ignoring architectural trends prevalent in the north, Florida's designers looked to the European origins of their state for inspiration, the result being a style of architecture loosely known as Mediterranean Revival: this embraced a wide range of sub-categories, from Italian Renaissance palazzo to Spanish Revival villa.

Outside Florida, architectural change and progress in the eastern United States in the first decades of the 20th century owed little to the building styles of pioneer ancestors, or even to the more recent influences of the Chicago School and Gustav

Stickley's *Craftsman* magazine. Of much greater significance were the practical requirements of America's rapidly growing commercial and industrial sectors.

When Frank Lloyd Wright designed the Larkin Building (page 262), what was uppermost in his mind were the special needs of people working in the relatively new mail-order business in an environment that, if badly ventilated and lit, could have caused workers to perform less effectively. In New York the need to house more and more commercial companies and their employees in the confined space of Manhattan Island led designers to find their own ways of using new materials – plate glass, steel, and reinforced concrete (the latter first experimented with in England but developed and given architectural cachet in France in the later 19th century) and new technologies in buildings that were climbing ever higher into the sky.

While the money and the get-up-and-go willingness to experiment with new ideas was wholly American – and the envy of European architects – much of the inspiration and materials connected with this building boom came from Europe. Here, before the First World War, artistic movements particularly relevant to architecture included German Expressionism, Art Nouveau and the Arts and Crafts Movement; after 1918 these were, if not totally replaced, then certainly modified by European Modernism and Art Deco.

The seeds of the Modernist movement in architecture had been sown in pre-war Europe by the work of men like the Austrians Otto Wagner and Adolf Loos, the German industrial architectural designer Peter Behrens and the Frenchman

OPPOSITE: Hotel and club, Roca Baton, Florida.

LEFT: Biltmore Hotel, Coral Gables, Florida (opened 1926). This and the hotel opposite are examples of the Mediterranean Revival style, popular in Florida, that grew out of the state's early European connections.

RIGHT: Frank Lloyd Wright's Taliesin West, Scotsdale, Arizona, begun in 1937 and expanded over many years.

FAR RIGHT: Empire State Building, New York (1930–31). Architects: Shreve, Lamb & Harmon. (See page 286.)

OPPOSITE: Chicago Board of Trade Building, Chicago, Illinois (1930). Architects: Holabird & Root. Scuptural details: Alvin Meyer.

Auguste Perret. These seeds came into flower after 1918, notably in the hugely influential work of Walter Gropius, founder of the Bauhaus School in Germany, and Le Corbusier (Charles-Édouard Jeanneret) in France.

European architects began to arrive in America in good numbers in the early decades of the 20th century, attracted by the boundless optimism and willingness to try out the new that was part of the American character, and by the technologically innovative work of architects like Louis Sullivan and his successors. Rudolph Schindler and Richard Neutra came from Austria and worked for a time with Frank Lloyd Wright before going on to design seminal houses of their own in California, while Mies van der Rohe and Le Corbusier were invited to America in the 1920s by Philip Johnson, then Director of the Architecture Department at New York's Museum of Modern Art.

It was Johnson, working with architectural historian Henry-Russell Hitchcock Jr., who was largely responsible for bringing the Modernist architecture of Europe to the forefront in America. Their Exhibition of Modern Art, mounted at New York's Museum of Modern Art in 1932, and the book that accompanied it, *The International Style*, the title of which was suggested by MoMA's director, Alfred Barr, gave the first period of 'modernist' architecture in America its name and its purposeful direction.

Modernism, be it 'European' or 'International', was not the only influential architectural style in America in the 1920s and 1930s. Art Deco, with its hallmark smooth and elegant curves, its zigzags and overlapping circles, seemed perfectly in tune with the Jazz Age of the 1920s – the era of the flapper girl, the luxury

OPPOSITE: Solomon R. Guggenheim
Museum, Manhattan, New York
(1943–59). Architect: Frank Lloyd
Wright. (See page 308 et seq.)

ocean liner, the New York skyscraper, stylish hotels of well-off vacationers, and silent movies – and the 1930s, the decade of the talkies and the Great Depression. Unlike the functionalist Modernist style, Art Deco was able to respond to society's need for fun, pleasure and an escape from the everyday world. It had a more serious side to it, of course, than mere frivolity. In the 1930s, elements of Art Deco and Modernism found a middle ground in a style nicknamed 'Streamline Moderne', when the straight lines of Modernist steel and glass buildings were given more fluidity and a degree of ornamentation.

Like 'International Modernism', the name 'Art Deco' derived from an exhibition, in this case the hugely influential Exposition of Decorative and Industrial Arts held in Paris in 1925, although the style had had its beginnings some years earlier, when the old pre-First World War Art Nouveau style had been recognized as out of step with the new age. Also in Art Deco's cultural background was Expressionism, the non-geometric free forms of which could be seen in the boldly sweeping curves given by architect Erich Mendelsohn to his Schocken Department Store in Germany and which, after he arrived in America in 1941, he used to greatest effect in his Maimonides Health Center in San Francisco (page 314).

Different from both International Modernism and Art Deco was the work of Frank Lloyd Wright, who designed some of his greatest buildings in this period, and whose work can be regarded as in a class of its own. To him, each building had its own particular requirements, leading him to vary his approach accordingly, while at the same time ensuring that it worked perfectly within its environment. Wright's open-plan Prairie House appeared early in the century, challenging the prevailing, traditional notion of what a home should be, while towards the end of his life came his extraordinary spiral Solomon Guggenheim Museum in New York. These, and the many Wright designs that came between, were all distinguished by the originality of the mind that had created them.

Whitehall
(Henry Morrison Flagler Museum)
Palm Beach, Florida
1901

This grandiose and ostentatious mansion was the winter retreat of Henry Morrison Flagler, the wealthy railroad magnate who, with John D. Rockefeller, founded the Standard Oil Company in 1870 and brought the railroad to Florida, thus establishing the Palm Beach season popular with the rich of America's Gilded Age. Flagler built Whitehall as a four-million-dollar wedding present for his third wife.

Flagler was well-versed in the art of creating impressive buildings, for his financial interest in Florida had not ended with the railroad, which reached St. Augustine in 1888, and Flagler decided to open his first luxury hotel in the city soon afterwards. Well aware of the value of history where tourism was concerned, together with a little romance, Flagler called his hotel the Ponce de León Alcazar and built it in the Spanish Renaissance style. He used the same formula for his Royal Poinciana Hotel, which, with its 540 rooms and its own stopping place for Flagler's trains, was one of the largest in the world when it opened in Palm Beach in 1894.

But even among the many grand hotels (there were 11 in all) that made up Flagler's hotel and railroad empire in Florida, Whitehall stands out from the crowd. Designed by John M. Carrère and Thomas Hastings, both of whom had trained at the École des Beaux-Arts in Paris, the house was built on a six-acre lot on Lake Worth, and when completed was described in the *New York Herald* as 'more wonderful than any

OPPOSITE & LEFT: Whitehall (Henry Morrison Flagler Museum), Palm Beach, Florida.

The Robie House, perhaps the most famous of the many houses that Frank Lloyd Wright designed for clients in and around Chicago, is regarded as one of the finest examples, even the apotheosis of the architect's Prairie House period from around 1887 to 1914. It was built for Frederick Robie, a manufacturer of machine parts and bicycles, near the site of the 1893 World's Columbian Exposition and is now on the campus of the University of Chicago.

A brick and sandstone building that incorporated several

OPPOSITE & THIS PAGE: Frederick C. Robie House, Chicago, Illinois.

the next two decades, during which time he was commissioned to design dozens of houses for clients in towns in Illinois, Wisconsin, New York, Indiana, Nebraska, Ohio, Iowa; in fact, throughout the prairies and beyond. The early style of these houses was characterized by overhanging roofs, an emphasis on the horizontal, and a marked asymmetry in their composition. These were single-family houses, recalling the typical North American farmhouse in their simple yet strong layouts, and were set in green surroundings.

wife, Elizabeth Barrett Browning, and a second-century Roman marble basin that was used in the loggia.

The house, on its 10-acre (4-hectare) site on Biscayne Bay in Coconut Grove, was surrounded by formal landscaped gardens, with parterres and much topiary work designed by Colombian landscape designer Diego Suarez. Scattered through the fabulously beautiful gardens were many fountains and sculptures.

Today Vizcaya is owned by Dade County, which has restored the house and its gardens and opened them to the public as the Vizcaya Museum and Gardens. It is one of the most enjoyable treats Miami has to offer.

San Simeon
(Hearst Castle)
San Simeon, California
Begun 1919

Such was the force of publishing magnate William Randolph Hearst's personality that it is easy to assume that his was the only hand at work in the creation of his garishly extravagant retreat in California's Big Sur. In fact, the famous architect, Julia Morgan (1872–1957), who had been the first woman to be admitted to the École des Beaux-Arts in Paris and the first to be awarded the school's certificate of architecture, was the major influence in the house's design.

When William Randolph Hearst began to plan a new house on the 30,000-acre (12000-hectare) ranch his father had bought high up on a coastal ridge overlooking San Simeon Bay, he simply envisaged something larger than the modest Craftsman-

OPPOSITE & LEFT: San Simeon (Hearst Castle), San Simeon, California.

RIGHT & OPPOSITE: San Simeon
(Hearst Castle), San Simeon, California.

style ranch house his father had built. But Hearst's mother had taken William on a grand tour of Europe when he was only ten years old, and the experience had obviously influenced him, if only subliminally.

When Hearst came into full possession of the San Simeon property on the death of his mother in 1919, he asked Julia Morgan, the Hearsts' favourite architect, to design him something in a 'Jappo-Swisso bungalow'-style, large enough to accommodate his family and guests in comfort. Morgan was equally at home with the Arts and Crafts Shingle style as she was with Spanish Colonial Revival, a blend of elements of the California missions and the vernacular architecture of the Mediterranean. But she – and Hearst – were possibly persuaded to choose the latter style, because it had become very much in vogue after a Panama-California Exposition in San Diego in 1915–16. Over the next 30 years or so, Hearst and Morgan created a sprawling complex of buildings covering 27 acres (11 hectares) that looked as though a prosperous Spanish hill town had been transported to the coast of California.

Dominating the San Simeon complex, with its three guest 'cottages' and outdoor Neptune Pool, surrounded by Classical colonnades and a Grecian temple, is Hearst's 100-room Casa Grande, or Great House. Built facing west towards the Pacific Ocean and rising cathedral-like over the rest of the estate in what Morgan called 'a fine "looming up" effect', Casa Grande is an earthquake-proof building of reinforced concrete faced with stone, in a style that is strongly Spanish Baroque. Two great towers rise above the front facade, which has a heavily ornamented main entrance surmounted by a cast-stone balcony.

Inside, Casa Grande is grand indeed. Since it would require an entire book to describe its glories, it must suffice to say that every room is crammed with the finest tapestries, ceilings, fireplaces, choir stalls, furnishings, books, Greek vases and rare objects that Europe had to offer a man with unlimited financial resources.

By the time he died aged 88 in 1951, Heart's 'bungalow', despite being unfinished, was one of the most famous houses in the world. Referred to as Hearst Castle in all the guide books, William Randolph Hearst's great house, officially the 'Hearst San Simeon State Historic Monument', attracts a million visitors a year, curious to see how one very wealthy American lived his colourful life.

Egyptian Theatre
Hollywood, Los Angeles, California
1922

When the famous impresario Sid Grauman's Egyptian Theatre opened on Hollywood Boulevard in 1922, it changed movie history. The first de luxe movie palace in Hollywood, the building was the absolute epitome of glamour and style, and the perfect setting for the very first Hollywood movie premiere – that of *Robin Hood*, starring Douglas Fairbanks – which took place there on 18 October 1922. Thus was ushered in, against a backdrop of ultra-fashionable Art Deco style, the era of star-studded, flashbulb-popping Hollywood celebrity that is with us still.

The art of Ancient Egypt, which was the decorative theme of the Egyptian Theatre, was one of the threads that ran

OPPOSITE:: San Simeon (Hearst Castle), San Simeon, California.

Egyptian Theatre, Hollywood, Los Angeles, California. Stained-glass detail.

through the wonderfully eclectic Art Deco style, and became even more significant after the discovery of King Tutankhamun's tomb near Luxor in November 1922. But archaeological discoveries in Egypt were not new: the world had been thrilling to them since the mid-19th century. Art Deco drew on generic, rather than particular Egyptian themes, with the sun, the lotus flower (and bud), scarabs, pylons, pyramids and hieroglyphics all being incorporated into the style. All these found places in the decorative scheme of the Egyptian Theatre, the use of the sun, in the form of an ornate sunburst ceiling in the auditorium, being perhaps the most impressive.

Sid Grauman fronted his Egyptian Theatre with a forecourt lined with palm trees that allowed him to display exotic set pieces from the movies he premiered there, such as Cecil B. DeMilles's colossal *The Ten Commandments* in 1923. This is still a feature of the Egyptian Theatre, which was restored to its original glory in the late 1990s.

The Egyptian Theatre in Hollywood is a fine example of the way America has learned to love and appreciate its old architecture, instead of putting something that might be more profitably exploited in its place. The theatre, which was closed in 1992, was rehabilitated and restored by American Cinematheque, a non-profit-making arts organization, with the help of the Community Redevelopment Agency. Its team of architects, acoustical and structural engineers, decorative painters and conservators, painstakingly restored the theatre to its full 1920s glamour, incorporating all the latest technology for the showing of films, while still retaining the period Wurlitzer organ to accompany silent films. In 2000, the scheme won an award from the National Trust for Historical Preservation.

As the home of American Cinematheque, the Egyptian Theatre presents a year-round programme of rare, unusual and classic films, documentaries, independent films and world cinema, as well as regular post-screening discussions between directors, actors and film historians. Sid Grauman would surely be delighted that his movie theatre is still fully engaged in the business of the 20th century's greatest art form. And he would probably not mind, either, that a great rival movie palace, Charles E. Toberman's Chinese Theater, which opened in 1927, is also still going strong.

**Ford Glass Factory
Dearborn, Michigan
1922**

The great contribution made by German-born Albert Kahn (1869–1942) to architecture in America, where he emigrated with his parents in 1880, was as a designer of 'perfect industrial buildings'. His Functionalist architecture, in which restrained design was tailored to the needs of industrial practice, anticipated in its precisely delineated cubic lines the work of such architects of the 1950s and 1960s as Mies van der Rohe and Eero Saarinen.

Kahn's neat and efficient buildings so impressed Russian industrialists visiting Detroit, where Kahn had his practice in the 1920s, that they invited him to Russia to work on a massive industrial building programme. He was in Russia from 1928 to 1932, during which time he designed not only the tractor factory in Stalingrad, that had been a primary reason for the invitation, but more than 500 other factories as well.

Outstanding among Kahn's work in America in the 1920s was the massive Rouge River factory at Dearborn, Michigan, that he designed for the production of sheet glass for the Ford Motor Company. The plant had four large melting furnaces, whose tall, slightly tapering brick chimneys, set side by side at one end of the factory, were the strongest element in its design. The building was essentially a long, symmetrically laid-out shed, and large sections of its mostly glass roof could be opened to release the heat that built up inside: this was considerable, since the factory was in operation for 24 hours a day.

The glass was cooled on conveyer belts set along the length

of the shed and, once cooled, the glass was cut and polished. During the whole cooling, cutting and polishing process, each piece of glass travelled the length of the shed three times. This, in effect, was a modern industrial process being carried out in a building designed specifically for it, not only with a knowledge of the principles of the process itself, but also of the precise architecture required.

In the 1930s, Kahn's practice in Detroit was involved in something like 20 per cent of all the new factories designed in America before 1939. His own last project was for a bomber factory in Omaha, Nebraska, the products of which were probably used against Germany, the country of his birth.

Ca' d'Zan
(John and Mabel Ringling Museum of Art)
Sarasota, Florida
1924–26

This splendid Venetian palazzo of a house was built by the wealthy circus impresario John Ringling and his wife Mabel as a winter retreat. They had been coming to Sarasota every winter since 1912, where they already had a frame house on a 38-acre (15-hectare) tract of land that they owned. Wealthy Americans had been putting their vast, lightly-taxed riches, gained from America's rapidly growing industries, into winter homes in the state since the 1890s, and John and Mabel Ringling decided to emulate them.

It had become a matter of pride with the wealthy in Florida to build in the grand style – in several grand styles, in fact, to which could be given the all-encompassing description of

'Mediterranean Revival'. John and Mabel Ringling decided to build in the Italian manner and commissioned architect Dwight James Baum to design a home in the style of a Venetian palazzo. They even gave it an Italian name, Ca' d'Zan, 'John's House' in Venetian dialect. Begun in 1924, it was finished in time for the Ringling family to enjoy Christmas 1926 in their new house, and when Ringling made Sarasota the winter quarters for his circus in 1927, they used Ca' d'Zan for two or three months every year.

The house that Dwight Baum designed for the Ringlings was notable for its lavish, no-expense-spared detail (such as 16th-century roof tiles from Barcelona) and fine craftsmanship, including expanses of fine decorative terracotta tilework, made at Crum Lynne in Pennsylvania. The part of the house that was most evocative of Venice was the 200-ft (60-m) terrace on the west facade, facing Sarasota Bay. From the terrace, Mabel Ringling was able to wander down broad, marble steps to her Venetian gondola, while John Ringling kept his 125-ft (38-m) steam yacht *Zalophus* moored nearby, ready to transport family and friends across the bay.

At the heart of the house was a vast living room, overlooked by an elegant gallery. A black-and-white marble floor, a coffered ceiling, and a chandelier from the old Waldorf Astoria Hotel in New York were notable features of the room. Hidden behind tapestries were the 4,000 pipes of a magnificent aeolian organ.

Today, Ca' d'Zan is at the heart of the John and Mabel Ringling museum complex, which includes a Museum of Art, the Ringling Museum of the American Circus, and the 300-seat horseshoe-shaped Asolo Theater, based on the 19th-century interior of the hall of a castle in Asolo, Italy. However, the theatre is no longer used as such, but for private lectures.

The John and Mabel Ringling Museum of Art – Florida's official art museum – contains many fine items, including several tapestry cartoons and two paintings by Rubens acquired by the Ringlings themselves. Among the fountains that play in Ca' d'Zan's bougainvillea-hung courtyard are displayed copies of famous Italian statues and other antiques.

Lovell Beach House
Newport Beach, California
1926

Austrian-born Rudolph M. Schindler (1887–1953) trained as an architect in Vienna, where he was greatly influenced by Otto Wagner, a leading theorist of the new Rationalism in European architecture at the turn of the century. In 1914 Schindler went to Chicago where, in 1917, he joined Frank Lloyd Wright's practice, and during the three years of their association absorbed much of the older architect's thinking on the relationships between architecture and society and the way in which these ideas could be realized in buildings, Wright's own houses in particular.

In 1920, Wright sent Schindler to supervise one of his projects in California. Schindler never returned, but opened his own office in Los Angeles in 1921, and practised there until his death in 1953. In California, Schindler's earlier influences were distilled into designs in which his resolution of the relationships between horizontal and vertical, and between

OPPOSITE: Ca' d'Zan, Sarasota, Florida.

solid and void, resulted in buildings that were distinctive and even revolutionary in their time.

The house Schindler built for himself in Los Angeles in 1923 was certainly in this category: a single-storey, timber-framed house in which the rooms of the minimally-designed, concrete-floored interior seemed to merge into one another and into the garden outside, which was to influence architects and designers for decades to come. The house was occupied by a succession of writers and artists after Schindler died, and is now a museum and a shrine to its designer.

One of Schindler's most architecturally satisfying buildings in California, and one that clearly showed the influences of European Modernism and of Frank Lloyd Wright, was the simple, inexpensive beach house built for Dr. Philip Lovell at Newport Beach in 1926. A neat exercise in space and structure, the Lovell Beach House was raised above street level on five exposed reinforced-concrete frames. This gave the house a covered open area in which there was a fireplace for open-air barbecues. Above it, the two-storey living room's front wall was predominantly glass, offering a magnificent view over the Pacific Ocean.

The cantilevered second storey of the house had stuccoed wooden parapets, behind which were the bedroom loggias, again with splendid views of the Pacific. The way in which Schindler used the small space of the beach-side lot to provide plenty of easy living space was an eye-opening lesson in modern-movement design that few American designers dared to emulate in the 1920s. Eighty years later, although somewhat altered from Schindler's original design, the Lovell Beach

House remains an intriguing and remarkably modern-looking building.

Lovell House
('Demonstration Health House')
Los Angeles, California
1927–29

Los Angeles-based Dr. Philip Lovell had a real interest in modern architecture, and could afford to commission the best. Only a year after he had taken possession of the beach house designed for him by Rudolph Schindler at Newport Beach, he asked another California-based architect, Richard Joseph Neutra (1892–1970), to build him a villa in Los Angeles. Dr. Lovell described the house, which was to incorporate family accommodation and an experimental open-air school, as a 'demonstration health house'

The Austrian-born Richard Neutra studied architecture in Vienna, where he knew both Erich Mendelsohn and Adolf Loos, a pioneer in the development of the European modern movement. Like Rudolph Schindler, Neutra worked with Frank Lloyd Wright after emigrating to America from Austria in 1923. He moved to Los Angeles in 1925, where he began his architectural career there in Schindler's office. He was already becoming known for designing private houses in a style that, in its emphasis on the relationship between volume and light, was moving steadily towards International Modernism, and the commission from Dr. Lovell was to prove a key point in the development of this style. Indeed, the Lovell House, along with Schindler's Lovell Beach House in Newport Beach, has been

OPPOSITE: Lovell Beach House, Newport Beach, California. Architect: Rudolph M. Schindler.

described as 'the greatest monument to the International Style in California'.

The site for Dr. Lovell's house was a steep hillside in the Los Feliz Canyon. Neutra designed a three-storey steel-framed house on a projecting reinforced-concrete foundation for this difficult site. It was given shape by an overlapping series of horizontal slabs and balconies supported by steel cables hung from the roof frame. Its surfaces were infilled with concrete and glass, and standard factory-built components were used throughout.

As the Lovell House was set below the road on which it was built, its main entrance was on the top floor. Its position also meant that only the back of the top floor of Richard Neutra's design could be seen from the roadway. To appreciate fully the architectural clarity of its lines, the observer really needed to be over on the other side of the canyon.

The Lovell House in California was contemporaneous with such European milestones in the development of International Modernism as Le Corbusier's Villa Stein in France and Mies van der Rohe's Barcelona Pavilion in Spain and shared with them a thin, weightless form, that only partly enclosed the interior spaces. Still as stylish and glamorous as it was when it was built, the Lovell House was given a starring role in the major Hollywood movie, *LA Confidential* in 1997.

Chrysler Building
Manhattan, New York, NY
1928–30

Automobile baron Walter P. Chrysler's eponymous skyscraper on Lexington Avenue took the 'World's Tallest' title from the

OPPOSITE: The Lovell House, Los Angeles, California. Architect: Richard Neutra.

LEFT: Chrysler Building, Manhattan, New York. Architect: William van Alen.

Woolworth Building when it was completed in 1930, and at 1,048ft (320m), the 77-storey building could have expected to have held the title for longer than a year. But skyscrapers were going up fast and high in New York at the time, and when the Empire State Building, with 25 more storeys, was completed in 1931, the Chrysler Building lost its crown.

As it happened, this loss of status mattered not at all, for nothing can challenge the Chrysler Building's role as a much-loved American icon of the Art Deco style. The building was the brainchild of Walter Chrysler himself, whose aim was to make his New York headquarters the tallest building in the world and a fitting symbol for his mighty Chrysler Corporation. He commissioned architect William van Alen (1883–1954) to create it for him, with the result that Chrysler – and New York – got was a masterpiece of steel technology and a work of flamboyant Jazz Age art.

From its base to the crowning peak of its seven-storey stainless steel-faced spire – deliberately designed to resemble the radiator grille of a car – the exterior of the Chrysler Building is pure Art Deco. Each of its stepped setbacks is decorated with objects resembling parts of cars, including wheels and radiator caps, while stainless-steel gargoyles, modelled on the bonnet ornaments of the 1929 Chrysler Plymouth, guard the base of the setback at the top.

The interior is even more stylishly and extensively decorated than the exterior. The stunning lobby, once used as a car showroom, is today one of the great New York interiors. It has walls faced with African marble, set in a symmetrical butterfly pattern and chromed steel-trimmed, while the vast ceiling is

covered with transportation scenes painted by Edward Trumball. Its elevators, worthy of a chapter of their own in any books on the elevators of New York, have doors and panelling covered with Art Deco marquetry. Visitors can see the lobby during office hours.

Although the Chrysler name remains firmly attached to the

OPPOSITE & THIS PAGE: Chrysler Building, Manhattan, New York.

building, the Chrysler Corporation never in fact occupied it, nor did William van Alen's reputation or fortune increase as a result of being its architect. Walter Chrysler accused him of numerous financial improprieties and refused to pay him, and Van Alen's career faded into obscurity.

Loew's 175th Street Theater (United Church)
Manhattan, New York, NY
1930

The silent movie, which reached a peak of popularity in the 1920s, led to a whole new style of architecture – a branch of theatre design uniquely peculiar to the cinema, while the coming of the talkies later in the decade saw new cinemas appearing at an unprecedented rate. Some of the most gloriously over-the-top of all cinemas were designed for Marcus Loew, a visionary theatre impresario who operated an enormous chain of cinemas in the 1920s and 1930s. Boasting that he sold 'tickets to theatres, not movies', he aimed to build movie palaces in as boldly glamorous and wonderfully decorated a style as his designers could envisage.

In 1930, at the height of both the Great Depression and the general enthusiasm for movie-going, Loew called in architect Thomas Lamb, who was something of an expert in the field, to design his 175th Street Theater in Washington Heights. The year before, Lamb had designed a movie theatre for Warner Brothers called The Hollywood, on West 51st Street, in the style of a Baroque cathedral with overtones of the elaborate fairytale palaces that King Ludwig II built in Bavaria before being eventually declared insane.

For Marcus Loew, however, Lamb produced an even more imaginative mix of architectural styles. Photographer/writer Joe Friedman described the lobby of the 175th Street Theater in *Inside New York* (Phaidon Press, 1992), as 'an Indo-Moorish fantasy, and a stylistic head-on collision between the Brighton Pavilion, Kajirao and the Alhambra'. He was struck by how remarkable the place must have seemed, at a time when very few Americans went abroad and could not have experienced any of these buildings for themselves.

Both of Thomas Lamb's late-1920s cinemas are now churches. Loew's theatre, with its spectacular lobby, auditorium and smoking rooms, still wonderfully preserved, is now the United Church, with services on Friday evenings and Sunday afternoons. The Hollywood, converted to both a theatre and a cinema in 1934 and renamed the Mark Hellinger Theater in 1949, is now the evangelical Times Square Church. Its interior, according to one of its preachers, in which 'you can feel the richness of God', was designated by the New York City Landmarks Preservation Commission in 1987 and its exterior in 1988.

McGraw Hill Building
Manhattan, New York, NY
1930

The building designed for the McGraw-Hill publishing company by New York architect Raymond Hood (1881–1934), who had studied at the Massachusetts Institute of Technology and the École des Beaux-Arts in Paris, certainly outshone its neighbours on West 42nd Street when it was completed in 1930.

The ground-floor main entrance was decorated in a dynamic

Art Deco style, elegantly striped in green, gold and silver, while beyond the entrance door, the lobby was decorated, again with stripes predominating, with opaque Carrera glass and stainless steel.

Outside, above the ground floor, the facade of the 35-storey building was faced with glazed terracotta tiles in an ultra-fashionable shade of blue-green, set between the horizontal stripes formed by large green metal-framed windows. This was a steel-framed building that shouted its basic construction to the world. There was no masonry cladding and no ornamentation on the outside: only the glazed terracotta brick tiles, the hues of which seemed to gradate as the building rose. Raymond Hood had been so concerned that the blue-green shade of the tiles should be consistent throughout, that he had personally inspected each batch of tiles as it was delivered.

In terms of its architectural style, the McGraw-Hill Building is transitional. It exhibits many signs of the later Art Deco style that came to be called 'Streamline Moderne', such as the blue-green tiles, the strongly horizontal lines and the strongly-marked setbacks, while the regularity of its facades, with their horizontal bands and terracotta panels, together with the lack of applied ornamentation, heralds the curtain-wall panels of International Modernism.

The great McGraw-Hill publishing company occupied the building for 40 years, maintaining its printing plant on the lower floors and its publishing offices and executive suites higher up. In the 1970s the company moved to new headquarters on the Avenue of the Americas and the McGraw-Hill Building, still retaining its original name, became offices.

Empire State Building
Manhattan, New York, NY
1930–31

As an example of early-20th-century New York architecture, the Empire State Building is not, at first sight, all that remarkable: just another steel-framed skyscraper encased in Art Deco styling. But it is one of the most famous buildings in the world. As the Eiffel Tower is to Paris and Tower Bridge to London, so the Empire State Building is to New York: an icon and a symbol as well as the centrepiece of the breathtaking New York skyline.

Because its opening coincided with the first major impact on American business of the 1929 Wall Street Crash, public reaction to the Empire State Building was relatively low-key. Nevertheless, it had 102 floors packed into its 1,250ft (380m) height, including a 150-ft (46-m) mooring mast for Zeppelins, and its height set a new world record. It was so difficult to rent out office space in 1931, however, that for a time the building was dubbed the 'Empty State Building', and it was only saved from bankruptcy because the observatories that had been built into it were immediately popular with the paying public.

But matters soon began to improve, partly because the Great Depression coincided with the great age of cinema in America. The 1933 film, *King Kong*, with its unforgettable climax in which the giant ape stands on the spire of the Empire State Building, swatting away aircraft as if they were flies, was just the first in a long line of films that helped to make the building familiar and famous throughout the world.

The Empire State Building was designed in the offices of the New York architectural practice of Shreve, Lamb & Harmon,

Empire State Building, Manhattan, New York. Architects: Shreve, Lamb & Harmon.

which conceived a building that could be constructed quickly and easily. Everything that could be was prefabricated, and the building went up at a rate of about four storeys a week. The framework, involving 60,000 tons of steel, was erected on more than 200 steel and concrete piles in less than six months. The building was lined with bricks — about ten million of them, while on the outside, aluminium panels replaced the more usual stone as surroundings for the building's 6,500 windows.

The building has grown since it opened, the mast having been increased in height to allow it to transmit radio and TV signals to the city and four surrounding states. It is now 1,472ft (450m) high, but very little of all this can be seen from the Fifth Avenue sidewalk in front of the building; this is because its eight-storey base hides the stepped-back floors above it from view. It remains a very public building, largely because of its viewing platforms, which have attracted some 120 million visitors since 1931. Once it was possible to see as far as 80 miles (125km) on a clear day from the 102nd-floor observatory, but this has been closed for some years, and today's visitors must make to do, like the romantic couple in *Sleepless in Seattle*, with the views from the outdoor observation decks on the 86th floor.

Rockefeller Center
Manhattan, New York, NY
1931–40

The size of New York's ambitiously conceived Rockefeller Center was such that it became as much an exercise in town-planning and landscape design as it was in architecture. The 12-acre (5-hectare) site in midtown Manhattan, bordered by Fifth

OPPOSITE & LEFT: Empire State Building, Manhattan, New York.

and Sixth Avenues to east and west and by 51st and 48th Streets to north and south, had been earmarked by its leaseholder, John D. Rockefeller, for a grand opera house in 1928. But the 1929 Wall Street Crash put paid to that idea, so Rockefeller decided to go ahead and develop the site in a rather more ambitious way.

Construction began in 1931 and by the time the Rockefeller Center had been completed in 1940, it had become the biggest privately-owned business and entertainment complex to have been constructed in the pre-Second World War period. It also provided work for 250,000 people at a time of deep depression, and was an exceptionally well-designed piece of urban planning.

Ten great steel-framed buildings, none of them technologically innovative but all good examples of skyscraper design, making use of the finest materials, including stone, granite and marble, were constructed between 1931 and 1940. One of the first buildings to be completed, which opened in December 1932, was the great Radio City Music Hall, a glittering Art Deco palace of entertainment, with an auditorium seating over 3,500. The last to be finished housed the offices of the National Cash Register Company.

Art Deco was in vogue when the Rockefeller Center was begun, and this was the style that was carried through to the last building, giving the complex cohesion throughout its design. Several of New York's leading architectural practices were involved in the design of the buildings, and in the commissioning of the works of art that adorned them. They included Reinhard & Hofmeister, Hood & Fouilhoux, and Corbett, Harrison & MacMurray. Raymond Hood, of Hood & Fouilhoux, the designer of the superbly Art Deco McGraw-Hill

OPPOSITE & THIS PAGE: Rockerfeller Center, Manhattan, New York.

Building, was in the forefront of the design work, notably in that of the Radio City Music Hall, while works by some 30 artists were commissioned for various buildings in the Rockefeller Center's foyers, facades and gardens.

More buildings were added to the Rockefeller Center after the Second World War, so that there were 19 buildings in the complex by the early 1970s. The Radio City Music Hall was completely renovated in 1999 and, restored to all its 1930s Art Deco glory, is the perfect host to many dazzling theatrical events.

Art Deco Style in Florida
South Beach, Miami
1920s–1930s

In 1979, an area of Miami's South Beach measuring a square mile, now called the Art Deco Historic District and containing more than 1,000 buildings, became the first to be added to the National Register of Historic Places in America in the 20th century. Thus one of the country's finest groupings of Art Deco buildings was saved from destruction.

Not all of the 1,000 buildings in the district are Art Deco, of course, but about 400 are, including private homes, hotels, theatres and shops – a dazzling array of buildings painted in a pastel rainbow of colours. For anyone interested in the Art Deco style this area of South Beach is a paradise indeed. It all began in the 1920s, when Art Deco and the beaches of Miami in winter time reached a peak of popularity simultaneously, which carried on well into the 1930s.

Not much is known of the quartet of developers and

OPPOSITE: Rockerfeller Center, Manhattan, New York.

LEFT: China Grill, South Beach, Miami, Florida.

entrepreneurs who built the Art Deco District, apart from their names: Albert Anis, L. Murray Dixon, Roy F. France and Henry Hohauser. But they certainly should be thanked for what they did for South Beach. Their aim had been to cash in as quickly as possible on the boom in winter vacationing, but they did it with style and with a standard of building and attention to detail that have enabled the buildings to weather 60 or 70 years remarkably well.

The buildings reflect the many different style categories within Art Deco. It is not surprising, perhaps, that a nautical style, rather like that of the great ocean liners of the period, is very much to the fore, with some buildings coming complete with porthole-shaped windows and tubular steel railings, such as

OPPOSITE & THIS PAGE: South Beach, Miami, Florida.

OPPOSITE & LEFT: South Beach, Miami, Florida.

RIGHT: South Beach, Miami, Florida.

OPPOSITE: Golden Gate Bridge, San Francisco, California, by Strauss & Morrow.

can be seen on the decks of ships. But elsewhere, notably along Ocean Drive, where many of the buildings date from the mid 1930s and later, there is much more of a Streamline Moderne look to the buildings. Take the Avalon Majestic Hotel on Ocean Drive, for instance, or – better still – the famous Marlin Hotel on Collins Avenue.

Since 1979 many Art Deco buildings have been saved and sympathetically modernized. Leonard Horowitz, a local designer, carried out much of the colour work, highlighting Art Deco features on buildings with a palette of colours that includes ice-cream shades of pink, green (ranging from eau-de-nil to sea-green) and yellow. It is no wonder that Miami's South Beach has become a magnet for moviemakers and fashion photographers and their models, as well as for holidaymakers looking for the ultimate in designer chic. There is even an annual Art Deco Weekend in Miami every January, celebrating the continuing fashion for winter vacations that started the whole Art Deco experience off in the first place.

Golden Gate Bridge
San Francisco, California
1933–37

Perhaps the best-known and best-loved symbol of San Francisco, the Golden Gate Bridge owes its existence and its elegant appearance to two men, its designer and engineer-in-chief Joseph Baerman Strauss (1870–1938), and its architect and technical advisor, Irving Foster Morrow (1884–1952).

The people of San Francisco had dreamed of a bridge over the Golden Gate strait, between San Francisco Bay and the

Pacific, since the mid 19th century, and it would certainly have facilitated communications between San Francisco and Marin County. However, it was not until 1916 that the city's leaders could be persuaded that a bridge of the necessary length (the Golden Gate strait was up to 2 miles/3km wide) might be a possibility. Many regarded it as unfeasible, while others said that, at an estimated cost of well over $100 million, it would be prohibitively expensive. Even when Joseph Strauss put forward a design, which he said would cost only around $30 million, complaints of local ferry operators that they would lose money, plus doubts about the structural integrity and aesthetics of Strauss's design, combined to get the idea shelved.

It did not stay shelved for long, however, and the project was approved in 1923–24. In 1928, the partly government-run Golden Gate Bridge Authority was established with the aim of getting the bridge built. Professor Charles Alton Ellis was brought in to validate Strauss's calculations, and Irving Morrow to make the bridge look more attractive. Strauss's scheme was accepted in 1930 and construction began in 1933.

Morrow's contributions were considerable. He lightened Strauss's original plan for huge towers by substituting the then fashionable Art Deco style and designed impressively solid concrete anchorages for the bridge cables that contrasted with the more delicate-looking steel structure of the bridge. It was Morrow, too, who gave the bridge its famous colour, by painting it 'International Orange'. The story goes that this was merely the undercoat, and that the bridge was intended to be an ordinary, practical grey. But local people liked the orange, so it stayed.

Once construction was under way, other engineers on the

project solved the structural problems caused, not unnaturally, by throwing a bridge over a tidal and stormy strait. Their answer was a cofferdam on the northern Marin Tower, and a massive fender standing in 112ft (34m) of water at the south tower.

The Golden Gate Bridge, with a main span of 4,200ft (1280m) and a total length of nearly 9,000ft (3000m), was the world's longest suspension bridge when it was officially opened by President Franklin D. Roosevelt on 28 May 1937, and other statistics connected with it were just as impressive. Because it spanned a major shipping lane, its roadway had to be 220ft (67m) above the water at high-tide level. The suspension cable towers were 500ft (152m) above the bridge deck, and the load of the main cables on each tower was 61,500 tons. All this took just 52 months to build and came in at only $5 million over Strauss's original estimate.

In the near-70 years since it opened, the Golden Gate Bridge may have long since lost its 'World's Longest' title, but over four billion vehicles and countless walkers have crossed it in that time, thrilling to its enormous size and the spectacular views it offers of the Northern California headlands and the great city of San Francisco.

Fallingwater
(Edgar J. Kaufmann House)
Bear Run Nature Reserve, Pennsylvania
1934–36

Of the many houses that Frank Lloyd Wright designed in his long and fruitful life, this is the one that stirs the emotions and imagination most. While a simple photograph or two can give an

idea of Fallingwater's brilliant effectiveness, only when it is seen in its setting, and walked around and through, can the variety of line, angle and changing perspectives, and the way the house sits so perfectly integrated within its natural setting, be fully appreciated.

Wright was well into his 60s when Pittsburgh businessman Edgar Kaufmann, owner of the city's leading department store, approached Wright and asked him to design a weekend house for him on land he owned on Bear Run Creek in the Laurel

OPPOSITE: Golden Gate Bridge, San Francisco, California.

BELOW: Fallingwater (Edgar J. Kaufmann House), Bear Run, Pennsylvania. Architect: Frank Lloyd Wright.

OPPOSITE & LEFT: Fallingwater (Edgar J. Kaufmann House), Bear Run, Pennsylvania.

OPPOSITE, PAGES 306 & 307: Johnson
Wax Building, Racine, Wisconsin.
Architect: Frank Lloyd Wright.

Highlands, south-east of Pittsburgh. A first look at the site told Wright that this was the one he had been waiting for all his life. As he was to tell students later, Wright felt that 'nothing ever yet equalled the co-ordination [and] sympathetic expression of the great principle of repose where forest and stream and rock and all the elements of structure are combined so quietly…'.

Legend has it that Wright designed Fallingwater in a day. He may well have done so, but before that day there had been a lifetime's search for a way to design buildings that married with nature and the environment in which they existed. With Fallingwater, Wright achieved the perfect merger of building and landscape into a complete whole.

Edgar Kaufmann's house was cantilevered out over a waterfall, and its several levels, pivoted around a central stone tower (the house's chimney), cascaded down the rocky hillside in a series of terraces. It seemed both to grow out of and remain a part of the swift-flowing rocky riverbed. The house was built of stone quarried from the property, and steel beams supported the concrete-walled terraces. Its interiors were also finished with rough stone walls and flagstone floors, while a large rock in the middle of the site was left to protrude through the living-room floor. As had been the case before, Wright designed the furniture for the house.

Kaufmann's son, Edgar Kaufmann Jr., entrusted Fallingwater to the Western Pennsylvania Conservancy in 1963, including in the donation all its Wright-designed furnishings and its artworks. Today, the only one of Frank Lloyd Wright's houses to have remained exactly as it was designed, Fallingwater is open to the public for ten months of the year.

Johnson Wax Building
Racine, Wisconsin
1936–39; 1944–50

In designing the headquarters for the Johnson Wax Company, Frank Lloyd Wright created yet another iconic 20th-century building. Or, more accurately, two buildings, because the Johnson Wax Building was designed and constructed in two stages First, between 1936 and 1939, came the main Administration Building, then, between 1944 and 1950 the Research Tower was added, intended for larger laboratory experiments.

The great red-brick complex, which like many Wright buildings ran enormously over budget, became one of his most dramatic-looking compositions and a study in geometric forms. This was due in large part to the contrast in the two main buildings: the Administration Building, its two parts connected by an all-glass tubular bridge, was low, rectangular and apparently windowless, and the squarer, round-cornered Research Tower rose 15 storeys and was sheathed in glass.

Herbert Johnson, like Larkin Company bosses before him, wanted his company's new administration building to be one that kept its workers' attention focused on the work in hand, not on what went on around them. Hence the lack of windows on the street side (in fact, there were light-diffusing bands of glass Pyrex tubing wired to steel frames at the top of each of the building's levels). The main illumination for the open-plan, galleried office space was a glass roof, or skylight, supported on mushroom-shaped columns, each designed to withstand a maximum of 12 tons and set 29ft (9m) apart. There was rubber

In designing the house, Goff worked closely with Ruth Vansickle Ford, a watercolourist and teacher at the Chicago Academy of Fine Arts, of which she was later president, and where Bruce Goff was also an instructor. The original inspiration for the design of the Ford House was said to have been a Tibetan nomad tent.

The Ford House was centred on a dome 166ft (51m) in circumference. Similar in construction to Quonset huts, which used corrugated metal, Goff built the house on a frame of red-painted steel, butt-welded to bent steel beams at the base. The dome, and a semi-circular dome annexe, were covered with shingles. A tall glass lantern, supported by a latticework of steel beams and set centrally over the dome, directed daylight right to the heart of the house.

Having a circular design, it is not surprising that the interiors of the Ford House were spectacular. There were two levels in the dome, with a galleried upper level reached by an open staircase, where a studio workroom for Ruth Ford was sited, and a dining and kitchen area beneath it at ground-floor level.

This was an imaginative house, designed by a man used to thinking outside the box, and it should have been wonderfully easy for the Fords to live in it. Unfortunately, it turned out to be too out-of-the-ordinary for the average citizen of Illinois, and their curiosity drove them in large numbers to the 'Round House', 'Umbrella House', 'Coal House' or 'Mushroom House', as it was variously called, to stare through its windows in amazement. In 1961, and nearing retirement, the Fords decided to sell their house and move into something more conventional.

Glass House
New Canaan, Connecticut
1949

Perhaps the most sophisticated glass box ever constructed, the steel-framed, transparent Glass House, designed by Philip Johnson (1906–2005), took the theme of the box in architecture into new territory – though it was territory into which the designs of Johnson's mentor, Mies van der Rohe, had shown the way. This highly individualistic house was placed in a park like setting against a backdrop of trees, its theatricality emphasizing that, rather than being a mere dwelling, it was a stage on which a lifestyle could be acted out. It has been called one of the 20th century's greatest residential structures.

Born in Cleveland, Ohio, Johnson chose to study philology at Harvard, but while there, he developed a strong interest in European avant-garde architecture, partly through his reading of an essay by the architectural writer Henry-Russell Hitchcock. At only 25, Johnson was appointed the first Director of the Architecture Department of New York's Museum of Modern Art (MoMA) in 1930. At MoMA Johnson became a major promoter of the Europeans, arranging visits to America by such leading European architects as Mies van der Rohe and Le Corbusier. His most notable promotional exercise was the first International Exhibition of Modern Architecture that he curated in conjunction with Hitchcock at MoMA in 1932, and which was accompanied by a highly influential book, *The International Style*, the title of which was suggested by MoMA's director, Alfred Barr.

OPPOSITE: Ford House, Aurora, Illinois. Architect: Bruce Goff.

OPPOSITE & LEFT: Ford House, Aurora, Illinois.

Glass House, New Caanan,
Connecticut. Architect: Philip Johnson.

In 1940, Johnson returned to Harvard to study architecture, alongside such influential architects as Walter Gropius and Marcel Breuer. For a time he had his own architectural practice in Cambridge, Massachusetts, but he returned to MoMA in 1946, and from 1954 until the end of his life practised as an architect in New York. It was while he was still at MoMA that Johnson designed and built the Glass House – not for a client, but for himself.

The Glass House is a 56 x 32-ft (17 x 10-m) rectangle. Its steel frame is painted dark grey and the steps and railing up to the door are of white granite. It does not sit alone in its setting, but is part of an architectural composition that includes a brick guest house and several pieces of outdoor sculpture.

The interior is completely open to view, the only out-of-sight element being the bathroom, hidden in the brick cylinder that provides the house's major spatial division; other space dividers are low walnut cabinets, one of which houses kitchen equipment and a free-standing 'buffet bar'. Both the cylinder and the red brick floor are waxed to enhance their dark purplish-red colour.

The influence of Mies van der Rohe, whose work Johnson greatly admired and had seen in many plans and designs, can be seen in the design of the Glass House. Here, on a small scale, is the archetypal Mies design – the glass box sustained by a concrete core containing the lifts that became the standard Modern Movement skyscraper style throughout the world. The Glass House represents the Modern Movement in perfect miniature.

General Motors Technical Center
Warren, Michigan
1955

Finnish-born Eero Saarinen (1910–61), who had come to the United States as a teenager with his parents, did most of his definitive architectural work in partnership with his architect father, Eliel Saarinen (1873–1950), in the latter's office in Ann Arbor, Michigan. Although Eero Saarinen achieved individual national prominence in 1948, with his winning design for the Jefferson National Expansion Memorial in St. Louis (not built until the early 1960s), and set up his own practice in Birmingham, Michigan in 1950, it was as a partnership with his father that he worked on one of the finest 'Saarinen' architectural groupings in the U.S., a technical centre for the giant General Motors Corporation.

The centre, a vast 330-acre (135-hectare) complex, eventually included 25 buildings set round an artificial lake. What General Motors had in mind was a business 'campus' – a revolutionary concept at the time. What they got was certainly a far cry from the rather grimly characterless city business and industrial districts in which so much of corporate America had grown up.

Drawing inspiration from the work of Mies van der Rohe, Eero Saarinen, working with his father, designed a series of low-rise, rectilinear steel-and-glass cubes notable for their geometrical and technological purity of line. Two far more Baroque elements – a large dome-shaped lecture theatre with a skin of aluminium and an aluminium, ellipse-shaped water tower – were set in the complex as a foil for the other buildings' straight lines.

Once in practice on his own, Eero Saarinen tended to return for inspiration to his early sculpture studies at the Grande Chaumière in Paris rather than to his father's more strongly architecture-based work. The near-Platonic purism of the General Motors Technical Center gave way to a much more mannered experimentalism, producing designs in a variety of styles with strongly sculptural forms. Among the most outstanding of these were the David S. Ingalls Ice Hockey Hall at Yale University (see page 335), the roof of which was suspended on both sides from a central concrete arch, and two airport terminal buildings, Trans World Airlines Terminal (1956–62) at Idlewild (now John F. Kennedy Airport), New York (page 350 et seq.), and the terminal at Washington, D.C.'s Dulles International Airport (1958–62). The latter was not completed until a year after Saarinen's early death in 1961.

Gateway Arch
St. Louis, Missouri
1963–65

When a competition was held in 1947 for a design for the Jefferson National Expansion Memorial in St. Louis, intended to commemorate the westward expansion of the United States in the 19th century, Eero Saarinen won it with a design for an elegant parabolic arch. His design drew on a project by the Italian architect Adalberto Libera (1903–63) for the entrance gateway to an international exposition planned for Rome in 1942, but which never materialized because the Second World War intervened. Saarinen's take on Libera's design won the competition but also had to await other world events before its

OPPOSITE: General Motors Technical Center, Warren, Michigan. Eliel & Eero Saarinen.

LEFT: Gateway Arch, St. Louis, Missouri. Eero Saarinen & Associates.

instance, evoked the curved lines of German Expressionism in the terminal he designed for Trans World Airlines at New York's Idlewild (JFK) Airport (page 350). And Buckminster Fuller, always a maverick where design was concerned, put the geodesic dome at the centre of several of his works, notably the Union Tank Company's Repair Shop in Baton Rouge (page 352) and the U.S. Pavilion at Montreal's Expo '67 (opposite).

As the 20th century progressed, Modernism came to be seen as more of a straitjacket than a source of inspiration. Issues concerning the environment had become more complicated than had been the case earlier in the century, when a shortage of city building land, coupled with the high price of that which remained, had been a major contributor in the development of the high-rise building. Now 'environment' meant rather more than saving land. Architects and designers were realizing that with its emphasis on the building as a functional 'machine for living', Modernism had a tendency to ignore the needs of the people obliged to live and work in such environments.

Kevin Roche's New York headquarters for the Ford Foundation (page 364) was an outstanding example of how to create a building that provided its occupants with ideal surroundings, complete with an indoor park, in which to work. Other designers began to abandon the pure lines of Modernism, sometimes by adding ornamentation to a basically Modern building, but, increasingly often, by abandoning the formal parallels of the style altogether. A new kind of architecture was beginning to emerge.

Museum of Modern Art
Manhattan, New York, NY
1939; 1953; 1984; 2002–04

New York's Museum of Modern Art (MoMA) was founded in 1929 but did not get its first permanent home, on West 53rd Street in midtown Manhattan, until 1939. In this year the

OPPOSITE: R. Buckminster Fuller's Biosphere, designed for Montreal's Expo '67, Canada

BELOW: Gateway Arch, St. Louis, by Eero Saarinen (see page 324).

museum was able to move into the first major public building in the International Style to be built on the east coast. This was entirely appropriate, since it was MoMA's founding director, Alfred H. Barr Jr., who had suggested the name 'International Style' for the book and exhibition on European architecture that Henry-Russell Hitchcock and Philip Johnson (1906–2005), first

director of MoMA's architectural department, organized in 1932.

Whereas in Europe architecture was as much concerned with politics and social philosophy as it was with pure style, in America style was everything – and perhaps never more so than when a museum of modern art was the subject under discussion. The six-storey building that the New York architectural practice of Philip L. Goodwin and Edward Durrell Stone designed for the Museum of Modern Art was a simple, clinical rectangular container. Its main, front elevation was extensively glazed, especially at the level of the two exhibition gallery floors above the entrance level, and formed a wall of glass through which natural light could be admitted. The library and office floor above were given more heavily-framed windows that could be opened, while at the top of the building, set back beneath a concrete canopy roof, were clubrooms with terraces. Down in the basement were a lecture theatre and cinema.

After the Second World War, MoMA grew rapidly and was regularly expanded, in the 1950s and '60s, to designs by Philip Johnson, who also designed MoMA's Abby Aldrich Rockefeller Garden in 1953, and in 1984 to the designs of Argentinian-born American architect Cesar Pelli, who created a controversial residential tower on top of the museum. However, museum space was still found to be inadequate, and in 2002 MoMA was closed and a large part of its collection was moved to a temporary home in Queens, while a major two-year renovation and rebuilding programme planned by Japanese architect Yoshio Taniguchi (chosen after an extensive worldwide search) was carried out.

MoMA re-opened in 2004, and the new six-storey glass-fronted David and Peggy Rockefeller Building facing 54th

Street doubled capacity to 630,000sq ft (58530m²). As with the original building, glass is used extensively in Taniguchi's new west wing, both on street-facing and on inner walls, giving visitors inviting views of areas such as the enlarged and restored Abby Aldrich Rockefeller Sculpture Garden at first-floor level.

While MoMA is still growing, the eight-storey Lewis B. and Dorothy Cullman Education and Research Building being not quite finished, this great museum of modern art is indeed, as Taniguchi has described it, 'an ideal environment for art and people [created] through the imaginative and disciplined use of light, materials, and space'.

MoMA's permanent collections contain more than 150,000 paintings, sculptures, prints, drawings, photographs and architectural models and drawings. There are over 22,000 films and something like four million stills in MoMA's cinema collection, with the classic films being shown in rotation in MoMA's refurbished Roy and Niuta Titus Theaters. MoMA's Library and Archives, with its 300,000-plus books, artist books and periodicals, provide valuable research facilities that are second to none.

Kaufmann House
Palm Springs, California
1946–47

The years immediately after 1945, marked by soaring demand for office space and domestic housing, produced some very innovative architecture in America. Outstanding among new housing designed at this time were the one-family villas designed by Richard Neutra (1892–1970) in California, especially those he was commissioned to build in the heart of the Californian desert landscape, away from the busy cities of the coast. The Kaufmann House, built in the desert against a backdrop of steep hills at Palm Springs, is perhaps the most famous of Neutra's later house designs. It was commissioned by Edgar Kaufmann, the same Pittsburgh businessman who had commissioned Fallingwater from Frank Lloyd Wright more than a decade earlier.

Although he did not go as far as Mies van der Rohe and Philip Johnson with their glass-box houses, extensive glazing was used by Neutra in the Kaufmann House, as was the case in his other villas of the late 1940s, notably the Tremaine House in Santa Barbara (1948). In the Kaufmann House, his use of glass, and of sun reflectors and mirror walls, was Neutra's way of fulfilling his constant goal that his buildings should fit harmoniously with their surroundings, be they urban or natural landscapes – a basic theme of International Modernism that was now just as important in post-war Modernism.

Since the Kaufmann House was to be a winter retreat for a wealthy man, it was both large and luxurious, and included servants' quarters. Designed as a series of elegant, precisely delineated horizontals, the house had walls that could be pulled back, so that the interior could be linked seamlessly to the exterior. Outside were spacious courtyards and a large swimming pool, reached by way of a broad, shallow flight of white steps from a terrace outside the main living areas.

A feature of Neutra's design was the way in which he

planned for the extremes of temperature likely to be experienced in the Californian desert. In the living area was a large fireplace, the rectangular white stone chimney of which was a dominant feature of the exterior view of the house, while the roof itself was coated with reflecting ceramic granules designed to reduce heat absorption. Pipes laid below the floors inside and the slabs of the terrace outside could carry either hot or cold water, depending on the temperature, and there were adjustable aluminium blinds to protect outdoor seating areas from sun and sand. These were sophisticated, modern solutions to age-old problems, and helped to make the well-planned Kaufmann House a masterpiece of mid-20th-century house design.

Farnsworth House
Fox River, Plano, Illinois
1946–50

Ludwig Mies van der Rohe (1886–1969) made his permanent home in the United States in 1937. He came from Germany, where he had taken over the directorship of the great Bauhaus school of art and design in 1930, only to have the position wrested from him when the Nazis, totally opposed to its radical modernistic teaching, closed the school in 1933. America with its architect community welcomed him with open arms – and clients with open wallets.

Mies was invited to teach at the Armour (later Illinois) Institute of Technology (ITT) in Chicago in 1938. He was already at work on his first large-scale commission in America, a plan for a campus and buildings for ITT, when he became involved in something very different: his first domestic commission. This was the Farnsworth House, designed as a weekend rural retreat for Dr. Edith Farnsworth at Fox River, Plano, Illinois.

Although small in comparison with the ITT project, the Farnsworth House was such a radical architectural concept that it took nearly five years to design and build. Because the site, in close proximity to the Fox River, was susceptible to flooding, Mies set the house, not on a foundation, but on terrace and main-floor platforms, the two connected by a wide flight of steps. The house was lifted above the ground on eight steel I-beam support columns. These were painted white, adding to the illusion that the house, with its glass walls and laterally-set terrace, was floating above the ground.

Essentially, the Farnsworth House was a single room, a box 77ft (23m) long by 28ft (8.5m) wide, and glazed from floor to ceiling. Inside was a centralized service core, clad in rare wood and containing the house's kitchen and bathroom, with a flexible space surrounding it, while the sleeping area was separated from the living space by a free-standing wardrobe.

In America, Mies virtually confined the design of his buildings to two forms. One was the skyscraper, which, in Mies's hands, was a skeleton structure clad in a seemingly unbroken glass facade, all the constructive elements of which were clearly displayed. The other, more low-rise in concept, was a building with a support-free interior that gave the impression of 'air between two plates'.

As a work of art, the Farnsworth House, transparently light and taut, yet apparently weightless, was the perfect example of this second concept. As a machine in which to live, however, it was considerably less satisfactory. Dr. Farnsworth felt she could no longer live there after a few months, finding it impossible to hang up a coat without having to consider how it would look from the outside.

Lake Shore Drive Apartments
Chicago, Illinois
1948–51

Mies van der Rohe's most famous dictum – 'Less is more' – could not have been put into practice more clearly than in the twin apartment blocks, startling in their simplicity, that he designed for construction mogul Herbert S. Greenwald at 860–880 Lake Shore Drive in Chicago. If Pietro Belluschi's Equitable Savings and Loan Association Headquarters (1948) had signalled the end of the between-the-wars era of the International Modern-style skyscraper in America, Mies van der Rohe's Lake Shore Drive Apartments confirmed that a 'third skyscraper age' had definitely dawned.

The years following the end of the Second World War were a time of boom for America, then enjoying a period of prosperity in sharp contrast to the situation that pertained in war-ravaged Europe. Once the economy and the building industry got into post-war gear, the demand for office space and private housing in America's cities was met by a new wave of skyscrapers, and apartment blocks soon became as high as the office blocks with which they shared expensive city development land.

The designs of Mies van der Rohe set the standard for these new skyscrapers, with their lightweight glass and metal walls and their regular, geometrical shapes. Where Mies had most dramatically departed from the pre-war International Style was in his insistence on simplicity and straightforwardness. His buildings were not only simplified, they were also organized in a pristine, perfect relationship between the proportions and the rhythms of their facades, on which the metal constructive elements, usually of a darker hue, were clearly visible.

Mies van der Rohe's two identical apartment blocks, set at right angles to one another on Chicago's Lake Shore Drive, heralded a dramatic change in building styles in the city, where not much had changed in terms of style since 1930. Each of the steel-skeletoned blocks was 26-storeys-high; with a ground plan ratio of three to five, these were not strictly towers. They were also not typical housing blocks: one of the main anti-Modernist criticisms of the Lake Shore Drive Apartments a few decades later would be that they looked like office blocks.

Once the buildings' skeletons had been completed, the prefabricated elements of the facade were lifted into position by cranes and welded together. The aluminium-framed windows, fitted in place from inside the buildings, were divided by Mies's trademark vertical metal I-beam projections, also used on the corner supports that rose the height of the buildings from the first floor. The central core of each building contained two lifts and a stairway, while car-parking space, storage areas and a laundry were hidden beneath each building.

The apartments are light and airy, with breathtaking views of Chicago and Lake Michigan from the plate-glass windows that fill their outer walls. Mies had originally wanted the apartments to be open-plan, but Herbert Greenwald preferred small rooms, believing they would be easier to rent out. When the apartment blocks were first opened, the lobby and the show apartments contained simple leather chairs designed by Mies himself. He also insisted the same-colour window blinds be used throughout, so that no obtruding colour or pattern would spoil the purity of his buildings' facades. While this perfect vision has long given way to the individual tastes, likes and dislikes of their occupants, the Lake Shore Drive Apartments remain a classic example of Modernist architecture.

Lever House
Manhattan, New York, NY
1952

Lever House, on Park Avenue in midtown Manhattan, was the breakthrough building that brought international recognition to the already influential architectural practice of Skidmore, Owings & Merrill (SOM). SOM began in 1936, when Louis Skidmore (1897–1962) and Nathaniel Owings (1903–84) set up in practice together in Chicago. In 1939, by which time the partnership had acquired an office in New York, John Merrill (1896–1975) had also joined the practice. From its earliest years, SOM operated on the lines of a well-organized American business, emphasizing teamwork and individual responsibility allied to a strict attention to good working methods and sound economic practice.

Gordon Bunshaft (1909–90), SOM's chief designer, was the creative impulse behind the 24-storey Lever House, commissioned by Lever Brothers as its headquarters building. The first of the city's light curtain-walled skyscrapers, it caused something of a

Lever House, Manhattan, New York.
Architects: Skidmore, Owings & Merrill
(Gordon Bunshaft).

sensation, not only because of its height, which, after all, was not all that great, but also for the way it reflected the other buildings on Park Avenue in its blue-green glass surface. A tall office tower slab occupying only part of the site's area and offset by the horizontal slab of its single-story mezzanine base, its innovative geometry and bright, crisp style ensured that Lever House would be copied again and again by architects all over the world.

Shining cleanliness being an essential in the headquarters building of the world's largest manufacturer of soaps and detergents, Lever House was given curtain walls of blue-green insulating glass, criss-crossed with slender chromed-steel mullions and transoms (and given the means to keep them clean in the form of rails for window-cleaning baskets that help to emphasize the building's verticals). The glass is translucent, except for bands of opaque glass used to identify the floors, with a strong band of opaque glass surrounding the top three floors of the vertical slab to hide the building's machinery. This top band not only balances the base slab, but also helps to emphasize the fact that it follows the basic design of Louis Sullivan and the Chicago School in being modelled on a Classical column, with a base, shaft and capital.

Lever House, currently squeaky clean following a recent major renovation programme carried out by SOM, is still occupied by Lever Brothers. It has public spaces that are open during office hours and its new Lever House restaurant is a place for VIPs to see and be seen.

By the end of the century, SOM, working from its five U.S. offices and others in London and Hong Kong, had completed over 10,000 projects in more than 50 countries, most of them in

the same smooth, lean style as Lever House, itself copied by other designers all over the world. Between 1954 and 1962, SOM designed the American Air Force Academy's new complex, high up on the edge of the Rocky Mountains at Colorado Springs. Its metal-clad chapel (1962) was designed by one of SOM's leading architects, Chicago-born Walter Netsch, and is an astonishing building, being a soaring folding of geometrical plates like aircraft wings, that reflect the shapes of the mountains in the distance.

Crown Hall, Illinois Institute of Technology
Chicago, Illinois
1952–56

Mies van der Rohe was commissioned to design the new campus and buildings for the Illinois Institute of Technology (ITT) shortly after he took up a teaching post there in 1938, when it was still called the Armour Institute. He began work at once on what was at the time probably the largest project of its type anywhere in the world. The geometrically-simple plan was finalized in 1940 and the first building was completed in 1943, by which time the United States had become deeply involved in the Second World War.

Although Mies was commissioned to design an academic campus, the fact that it was set on many acres in countryside on the outskirts of Chicago meant that it actually became the prototype for a new kind of commercial building, that would be in demand once the war was over: the prestige company headquarters building, preferably built not downtown but in a landscaped countryside setting out of town.

Mies van der Rohe's buildings for the ITT campus were

RIGHT & OPPOSITE: Crown Hall, Illinois
Institute of Technology, Chicago,
Illinois. Interiors.

notable for their designer's insistence on a sparing simplicity and for their rejection of anything that hinted at architectural individuality or artistic expression. It was, perhaps, a sign that his own instinct for the simple had been reinforced by too close a proximity to Chicago's many post-Chicago School buildings, that had lost sight of the original aims of the school in a welter of quick, cheap construction and poor design that left appearance unrelated to structure.

Simple lines and clearly visible metal frameworks characterized buildings on the ITT campus from the beginning. The Alumni Memorial Hall, completed in 1946, about the same time as the nearby Metallurgy and Chemical Engineering Building, had its concrete frame (required by fire regulations) masked in steel and brick, so that there was no hint of the concrete beneath. The building aroused worldwide interest.

As did Crown Hall, which housed ITT's School of Architecture and Design, when it was completed in 1956. Crown Hall's main level is a single space measuring 120 x 220 x 18ft (37 x 67 x 5.5m), enclosed in panels of both clear and opaque glass and steel. Such a large, completely open space was made possible because the roof was suspended from four exposed rigid plate girders. The girders were factory-made, each one delivered to the site in two 60-ft (18-m) sections.

Crown Hall has been criticized for its great open space, but the students who have lived with it over the past half-century all seem to view it with enthusiasm, which is what counts in an academic building.

Seagram Building
Manhattan, New York, NY
1954–58
Where skyscrapers were concerned, Mies van der Rohe contributed two classic works to American Modernism. One was

the Lake Shore Drive Apartments in Chicago; the other the Seagram Building in New York, designed in collaboration with the American architect Philip Johnson and completed eight years after the Chicago skyscrapers.

Samuel Bronfman, the president of Seagram, the Canadian gin distillers, was planning a relatively modest and ordinary building for his company's New York headquarters, when his architect daughter, Phyllis Lambert, persuaded him to commission Mies van der Rohe for its design. The result was something very far from modest and was way out of the ordinary. In fact, Mies van der Rohe gave the Seagram company a masterpiece of world architecture.

The 38-storey Seagram Building, with its clearly articulated planes and angles, is architecture at its most purist and abstract, both outside and in. The steel, I-beam-framed, bronze-clad building, presenting its broad side to Park Avenue from the far side of a smoothly simple and uncluttered entrance plaza, rises like a shining, gold-bronze cliff of glass from the midst of the lesser buildings that surround it. With it, Mies abandoned the 'pure box' concept, designing its rear facade to project at the centre by one support bay, and adding other elements in staggered steps on the side streets.

The lobby, inside the front, Park Avenue entrance, was designed by Philip Johnson in association with Mies. Like the outside of the building, the lobby, a virtually bare space, takes architectural design down to its fundamentals: line and perspective in a space. Dominating the head of the lobby's stairway is a theatre curtain by Picasso – a work of modern

art, but from the beginning of the period that culminated in the Seagram Building. Philip Johnson was also responsible for the landmark décor of one of the Seagram Building's most famous public places, the ultra-exclusive Four Seasons Restaurant. But Johnson was no longer in purist abstract mood when he made his designs for the restaurant. Its Pool Room has a palm-fringed pool and the Grill Room a bar that serves as a plinth for an arresting sculpture by Richard Lippold.

This was the first building Mies designed for New York and the largest of its type in the world when it was completed. It was also very expensive to build: the property developers' quip that 'Mies means money' could be taken two ways. However, because it occupied a relatively small space for its size, it had taken up a correspondingly modest piece of New York's exorbitantly-priced building land. Incidentally, Mies would not have been able to set the Seagram Building on its elegant plaza if the building regulations that came into force in midtown Manhattan in 1982 had been in place in the 1950s. In order to preserve the continuity of the lines of buildings unbroken, plazas were no longer acceptable after that date.

If the Seagram Building had a fault in 1958 it was that it looked too simple – just a vertically accentuated rectangle, after all – and therefore easy to copy. It isn't – as the hundreds of dreary and boring skyscrapers designed in the following decades demonstrate only too well. If the Seagram Building does not stand quite alone as a landmark of modern architecture, it still has few to equal it among its many imitators.

BELOW & OPPOSITE: Trans World
Airline Terminal, JFK Airport, New York.
Architect: Eero Saarinen.

Trans World Airline Terminal
JFK Airport, New York, NY
1956–62

Eero Saarinen (1910–61) always maintained he had a feel for the 'jet age', and this is surely confirmed by his two great air terminals, the Trans World Airline (TWA) building he designed for New York's Idlewild (now JFK) international airport and the Terminal Building at Dulles International Airport at Chantilly (near Washington, DC) in Virginia.

Both buildings offered special challenges to an architect: that of Dulles was that it was a new airport and a gateway to the nation's capital, being built for the Federal Government, while that of the TWA Terminal was that it was to be a showcase for a great airline in a highly competitive business, offering to America's – and the world's – rapidly growing 'jet set' a style in air travel that other airlines could not match.

Saarinen, in confident 'building stylist/engineer' mode rather than that of an architect, gave TWA an iconic building that resembled a bird poised for flight. The fluid forms, like the curves of a bird's wings, that dominated the lines of the building's exterior, and created dynamic, organic interior spaces beneath a soaring roof, were in sharp contrast to the clean lines of modern architecture in its purist form. It was as if Saarinen were abandoning American Modernism and looking to Europe for inspiration – to the more recent dynamic reworkings of space and form of Le Corbusier, and to the work of the architectural Expressionists of Austria and Germany before him.

Saarinen, whose aim was to make the TWA Terminal seem as though it was about to rise into the sky, gave its passenger area a dramatic reinforced-concrete roof composed of four arched shells supported on four Y-shaped columns. The gaps between the curves of the roof arches and its buttresses were glazed, allowing plenty of light into the building. Saarinen was not content to design just the shell of the building. The shapes of what was inside it were just as important in creating a pleasurable visual experience. As he himself wrote at the time, 'all the curves, all the spaces and elements... the signs, display boards, railings and check-in desks were to be of a matching nature'.

Certainly, Saarinen's Trans World Terminal matched the spirit of 1950s America perfectly. Since the demise of TWA in 2001, however, the terminal has since been closed, though plans are afoot to partially integrate Saarinen's structure into an expanded terminal for another airline.

Union Tank Car Company Repair Shop
Baton Rouge, Louisiana
1958

Richard Buckminster Fuller (1895–1983), an entrepreneur-inventor rather than an architect in the strict sense of the word, nevertheless made his mark on American architecture. One of his early, much-admired inventions was his Dymaxion House design of 1927, industrially-manufactured houses that took their name from the concept behind them: 'dynamic plus maximum efficiency'. Basically a collection of mechanical services joined to living areas, these really were 'machines for living in'.

Fuller later became interested in structures, particularly domes, and came up with something he called geodesic domes. Based on octahedrons or tetrahedrons, these could be built in metal or plastic or even cardboard. The dome shape interested him, not because of any lurking admiration for Classical or Greek Revival architecture, but because of the natural efficiency of the shape: it provided an optimum enclosed space in relation to the surface area of the enclosing form. In addition, the dome's parts could be manufactured in a standardized, assembly-line form, thus increasing the efficiency of the system and also making it easy to maintain.

While Fuller's dome design for the U.S. Pavilion at Expo '67 in Montreal (page 336) is probably his best-remembered, the one he produced a decade before for the manufacturer of railway wagons, the Union Tank Car Company, at Baton Rouge, certainly deserves a leading place in the history of American architecture. The dome was vast and was designed to house the company's repair shop, having a diameter of 384ft (117m). It was the largest dome to be designed by Fuller and the largest circular structure in the world at the time, Ralph Tubbs's Dome of Discovery built for the 1951 Festival of Britain having by now been pulled down. Fuller's was built from lightweight hexagonal steel sections that were lifted into place by cranes.

The Union Tank Car Company Repair Shop was as high as a ten-storey office block and had room inside for a full-size football pitch – or this would have been the case if Fuller had not put a smaller, 80-ft (24-m) diameter open dome inside to act as the service operations centre and site of the major repair unit. A 200-ft (60.5-m) long connecting tunnel led from the main dome and, also covered in hexagonal steel sections, was used as the paint shop.

So pleased was the Union Tank Car Company with its efficient, easily-maintained domed facility that it had another one built for it at Wood River, Illinois, in 1961.

Marina City
Chicago, Illinois
1959–64

By the late 1950s, Western architects and city planners were having to adapt to a rapidly changing world. The post-war baby boomers would soon be looking for somewhere to live in the rapidly growing cities that offered them the best jobs, while building land in those cities was becoming scarce and expensive. Marina City was one man's response to the urgencies of urban redevelopment in Chicago.

LEFT, PAGES 354 & 355: Marina City, Chicago, Illinois. Architect: Bertrand Goldberg.

Chicago-born Bertrand Goldberg (1913–97), who studied at Harvard and at the Bauhaus in Germany, was a classic Chicago architect. He believed firmly in the importance of architecture in society and that organic truths regarding architecture could be drawn from nature, while using every technological advance available. Goldberg has been called the city's 'great poet of the urban community', and Marina City is regarded as the finest work of his career.

Marina City consists of two cylindrical tower blocks – bearing a resemblance to corncobs, according to some – each of which provides apartments and plenty of car-parking space. Built in Goldberg's favoured material, reinforced concrete, with reinforced-concrete central cores to house utilities, the 684-ft (208-m) towers were the tallest reinforced-concrete structures in the world when they were completed. The utility towers were built first, and were so slender that they swayed in the wind. Goldberg constructed them 'slip-form' – a system that allowed the cores to be virtually their own cranes – then used them as armatures for the rest of the buildings, in much the same way that sculptors build up their clay sculptures.

Each tower contains 450 apartments, the floor plans of which extend from dense centres, like the petals of a flower, to the curving tips of their open balconies. The apartments are on the towers' upper 40 floors, and there are 20 floors of car parking below them, spiralling down to the horizontal bases of the towers, where there are shops, restaurants, an ice rink and a health club. Other elements in the make-up of Marina City are an office block, a theatre and a marina on the river, where the flat-dwellers above can moor their boats.

RIGHT: Marina City, Chicago, Illinois.

OPPOSITE & PAGE 358: Salk Institute of
Biological Studies, La Jolla, California.
Architect: Louis Kahn.

Marina City, built riverside at 300 North State Street in urban Chicago, is just that: a city within a city. It is a vibrant, lively, densely-packed community where urban living is something to be enjoyed rather than endured, as was the case with so many other tower blocks going up around the same time as Marina City.

Salk Institute of Biological Studies
La Jolla, California
1959–65

Dr. Jonas Salk invented a successful vaccine against poliomyelitis in 1953 and chose to put the proceeds from it into an institute devoted to medical, especially cancer, research. Salk conceived his institute as having three main elements: research laboratories, a meeting and discussion facility, and living quarters for students, resident scientists and assistants. He also wanted a library with reading rooms and places for social gatherings. The Estonian-born, American-trained architect Louis Kahn (1901–74) had recently shown his designs for the Alfred Newton Richards Medical Research Laboratory for the University of Pennsylvania at the Museum of Modern Art in New York, where they had aroused tremendous public interest (the building was completed in 1960) and Salk decided that Kahn was the man for the job.

The site chosen by Salk for his institute was sensational: set on high ground, scattered with cactuses, lemon trees and other shrubs, it overlooked the Pacific Ocean, and there was a deep canyon running through it from east to west. This was not an easy site for an architect to work with, even before he

began to grapple with the special problems of building in an earthquake zone. Finalizing the designs took many months, partly because Dr. Salk had so many ideas of his own, many of which departed from the traditional academic type of building — but then, so had Kahn's ideas for the Richards Laboratory, but eventually the designs were complete.

Kahn designed the institute essentially as a two-winged complex, set on either side of a central paved courtyard or plaza. In each wing were laboratories, free of supports and undivided. Projecting from each wing towards the central plaza were five towers, housing studies and offices. Each tower was designed with two 45-degree diagonal walls that formed bays, one for each study, with views across the ocean. A narrow channel set in the centre of the plaza formed a linear fountain, the water in which fell by a series of steps down the lower levels of the complex towards the sea.

The overriding characteristic of Kahn's complex is its simple, straight-lined sculptural quality. It is an effect achieved by the combination of bare, geometrically shaped surfaces and the materials that Kahn used, especially concrete and travertine. The concrete was given a warmer colour than usual by mixing several different types with other ingredients, including pozzolan. The nature of the site meant that pre-cast pieces could not be used – there was not enough space in which a large crane could work – and the concrete all had to be poured on site. Earthquake-proofing was complex and was achieved in part by using lead-zinc-covered steel plate interfaces between trusses and supporting columns and by providing joints with some stretch for the framing.

The Salk Institute in La Jolla is one of the great academic/research buildings of the 20th century. With its open laboratories, modular planning and ease of communication between its various elements, it is, to quote a scientist who worked there, a 'watershed laboratory of our time'.

Greene House
Norman, Oklahoma
1960–61

At first sight, Herbert Greene (born 1929) is unclassifiable as an architect. Take the house he built for himself in Norman, on the wide prairies of Oklahoma. Is it modelled on a bird? Well, it seems to have a beak, and its cedar shingles, wooden boards and corrugated metal pieces look like feathers... But Greene himself wrote that his house contains 'impressions of a large object, thing or creature, rather at home on or accommodating itself to an expanse of natural prairie', and there are two beak-like projecting elements which could be horns. So was the model for this extraordinary dwelling a buffalo, perhaps? Whether bird or buffalo, or, as it has also been called, armadillo, praying mantis, or (quoting Greene again) a mother hen protecting her young, perhaps the important thing is that they are all living creatures, products of nature – which brings that difficult-to-summarize form, organic architecture, into play.

Greene's great hero was Bruce Goff (1904–82), Dean of the School of Architecture at the University of Oklahoma in Norman and renowned for the exuberant eccentricity of his built work, mostly houses. Goff had been a pupil of Frank

Lloyd Wright, creator of the Prairie House (which Greene's house has also been called), who used the phrase 'organic architecture' when talking of the importance of uniting the form and function of a building and of ensuring, when designing it, that each part was both unique and inseparable from the whole. Wright, in discussing architecture in such terms was expanding the simple phrase of his own hero, Louis Sullivan, of 'form follows function'.

Seen in this context, Herb Greene's work, so far from being unclassifiable, fits into the broad pattern of thinking about architecture in terms of the relationship between function, site and the surrounding landscape that is called organic architecture. The creature-like form of the Greene House, built out of bits and pieces of readily available materials and set on the flat, treeless Oklahoma prairie, with its covered, tail-shaped walkway up to the entrance, is surely Greene's personal response to its siting.

The interior of the Greene House is as extraordinary as the exterior. The walls and ceilings, curving round and up and making odd angles, are covered in the same cedar shingles as the exterior, and there are a stone staircase and a wooden ladder reaching to upper levels. Lights are set in alcoves and in gaps cut through the walls. It is as if every rule of formal design has been set aside in the design of the house.

In recent years, Herbert Greene has had a big influence on the organic architecture school that grew up around the Hungarian architect Imre Makovecz, despite the disapproval of the Communist government, and which has seen a flowering in the post-Communist era.

John Hancock Center
Chicago, Illinois
1965–70

Chicago's Michigan Avenue was nicknamed the Magnificent Mile by a property developer in the 1940s, partly for its apparently endless line of upmarket department stores and partly for its many great office towers and skyscrapers. The real colossus of the Magnificent Mile – it is referred to by Chicagoans as 'Big John' – is Skidmore, Owings & Merrill's John Hancock Center, at 875 North Michigan Avenue.

Instantly recognizable from the criss-cross braces in its outer frame – designed to prevent the 100-storey building from swaying too much in the strong winds that blow in off Lake Michigan – the John Hancock Center is popular for the unrivalled views it offers both Chicagoans and visitors to the Windy City. From the Skydeck Observatory and the restaurants and bars that occupy the Center's 94th to 96th floors, there are spectacular views for 80 miles (129km) in all directions, both of Chicago and of four surrounding states, depending on the weather, of course.

For those more interested in architecture than eating, drinking and seeing panoramic views, the John Hancock Center has plenty of facts and statistics to offer. To begin with the background: it was built at the end of a decade during which the centre of Chicago had seen great changes in its population mix. Racial tension and urban decline had accelerated a move from the city centre to the suburbs on the city's outskirts, both by the resident population and by business, with shopping malls and industrial parks drawing

business away from the Loop. 'Big John' was the first large-scale multi-functional complex in the centre of Chicago and was seen, not simply as another trendy monolith, but as an affirmation of the continuing importance of the city of Chicago.

It is its engineering as much as its architecture that makes the John Hancock Center so dramatically impressive a building. From its early days, Skidmore, Owings & Merrill included engineers on its design teams, and it was its Chicago office engineer, Fazlur Khan, who developed the self-supporting 'tube construction' system that made very high buildings economically possible. This system gave tall buildings a strong self-supporting external frame, which, in the case of the Hancock Center, involved steel cross-braces criss-crossing their way up the building.

The John Hancock Center, occupying only 40 per cent of its 100,000-sq ft (9290-m²) site and situated some way from the Loop and near Lake Michigan, is almost another city in itself. The complex includes five floors of commercial spaces and offices, parking for 1,200 cars on floors above the offices, and 670 apartments on the floors above the 43rd.

Above these are the observatory, restaurants and bars, plus a History Wall and a virtual reality Windows on Chicago tour of 80 sites at the press of a button, to which visitors are whisked in high-speed lifts. All this in a 1,107-ft (337-m) vertical slab, tapering towards the top, clad in black anodized aluminium and glass, its frame enlivened by those great crossed steel braces.

John Hancock Center, Chicago, Illinois. Architects: Skidmore, Owings & Merrill.

Habitat
Montreal, Quebec, Canada
1966–67

The great world fair held in Montreal, Canada, in 1967, inspired much innovative architecture, including Buckminster Fuller's United States Pavilion, which was essentially a giant geodesic dome, 200ft (61m) high, composed of hexagonal units (page 336). The Israeli-born, McGill University graduate architect Moshe Safdie (born Haifa, 1938) contributed something that is still one of the architectural highlights of Montreal. This was his dwelling complex ('apartment block' in everyday terms), 'Habitat', intended to be permanent rather than something erected merely for Expo '67.

Habitat was Safdie's answer to the question that the architect Le Corbusier had posed and then answered just after the Second World War with his brilliant and still much admired Unité d'Habitation (1945–52) in Marseilles, France: how to prevent modern densely packed housing complexes, made up of prefabricated elements, from becoming soulless piles of concrete containers and so intimidating, with their dark corridors and ill-lit walkways, that their occupants are afraid to step outside their own apartments. Safdie, still in his 20s and recently installed in his own studio after a period of working with Louis Khan in Philadelphia, designed Habitat to provide 'privacy, fresh air, sunlight and suburban amenities in an urban location' and originally intended to include 1,000 apartments on the site. In the event, Habitat contains only 158, built from 354 independent prefabricated boxes, based on 15 different plan types, and connected by steel cables. Habitat is an extraordinary ziggurat of projections and recesses organized to give each apartment a private balcony or terrace, built on the roof of the apartment immediately below.

There are no long corridors or walkways in the ten-storey-high Habitat (there is a below-ground-level floor for machinery and a vehicle entrance). The units are built in three clusters, each with its own garden entrance and independent lift shaft and stairwell. The clusters are connected by horizontal shafts and 'streets' inside the complex. The structural engineer who advised Safdie on integrating the vertical and horizontal components of the structure was August Komendant, a colleague of Louis Khan, whose input had been crucial in the building of the Salk Institute of Biological Studies at La Jolla, California.

Each apartment in Habitat is made up of one, two or three prefabricated modules (made in a temporary on-site factory) measuring $17\frac{1}{2}$ x $10\frac{1}{2}$ft (5 x 3m) and each with a subfloor, where mechanical services such as piping and wiring are located. Bathrooms and kitchens were also prefabricated and dropped into place once each apartment was ready for them. Safdie intended Habitat to be not only an alternative to high-density suburban housing, but also an example of how modern, technologically-advanced housing can mirror the community-based hill towns of the Eastern Mediterranean, the region of his birth, even when densely packed.

While his later career took him back to the Middle East, Moshe Safdie was not lost to Canadian architecture and he has designed several important civic buildings in Canada since. The country celebrated the 125th anniversary of the National Gallery of Canada in Ottawa in 1988 by giving it a new home, a

OPPOSITE & PAGE 364: Habitat, Montreal, Quebec. Architect: Moshe Safdie.

splendid L-shaped glass and granite edifice designed by Safdie (page 399). The focal point of the gallery is the vast, multi-level Great Hall, whose soaring glass ceiling and walls were designed to echo the contours of Ottawa's historic Library of Parliament nearby. Light, spacious galleries, the amount of sunlight in them controlled by electronically-operated blinds and diffusing lenses, and quiet courtyards, lead visitors through the displays of Canada's richly diverse cultural heritage.

Ford Foundation Building
Manhattan, new York, NY
1966–68

The prestigious Ford Foundation's headquarters building, on Second Avenue between 42nd and 43rd streets, was unconventional in the extreme among Manhattan's sky-reaching towers when it opened in 1968. To begin with, it was only 12 storeys high (with a basement level below ground), and the amount of land left unbuilt on was extravagantly generous, nearly a third of an acre of the site being an indoor park.

The Ford Foundation Building is a perfect example of form fitting its function, which is to house the staff directing the work of one of the world's major philanthropic organizations. Its principal designer, Kevin Roche (born 1922), who had worked with both Mies van der Rohe and Eero Saarinen and was now partner in Kevin Roche, John Dinkeloo & Associates, was concerned from the outset that the building's environment should allow workers to be aware of each other, as if part of a working family, and to share in promoting 'the aims and intentions of the group'.

Ford Foundation Building, Manhattan, New York. Architects: Roche, Dinkeloo & Partners.

OPPOSITE: Kimbell Art Museum, Fort Worth, Texas. Architect: Louis Kahn.

of the 20th century's most innovative architects, Mies van der Rohe. It is all the more fitting, therefore, that in designing Lake Point, its architects, Schipporeit-Heinrich Associates, who had been former students of Mies at ITT, should look for inspiration back to one of his great unrealized projects of the 1920s, a 'free-form' glass-clad office block.

Lake Point Tower, made possible by the kind of glass and steel technology, plus American money and know-how, that were not available when Mies sketched his 1921 design, stands like an outsized glass lighthouse 645ft (196m) high on the shore of Lake Michigan. Planned as high-density housing for a prosperous clientele in an urban environment, the tower contains 900 well-appointed – and therefore expensive – apartments, two floors of commercial offices, and other adjuncts to good living, such as shops and restaurants.

The tower's curved plan and glazing, set flush so that it appears skin-like on the building, enables it to catch the sunlight all day, and looks as though it is on fire at sunset at the end of a fine day. Its residents, enjoying fabulous views from their eyries high above the busy city, have in recent years had something more interesting, or possibly more alarming, to observe below.

Navy Pier underwent a facelift in 1995 and its subsequent renovation has turned it and much of the area of central Chicago between Michigan Avenue and the lake into one of the city's most popular tourist destinations. Many shops and restaurant-chain eateries, an IMAX cinema and a 15-storey Ferris wheel are now in evidence, while the pier itself, as well as being an embarkation point for boat tours of the lake, is a concert venue and a site for weekend festivals. It is all much

livelier and noisier than it was when Lake Point Tower was first completed, when it could be seen as a monument to the restrained and elegant minimalism of Mies van der Rohe.

Kimbell Art Museum
Fort Worth, Texas
1967–72

Louis Khan once said that, of all his work, the Kimbell Art Museum was the building that satisfied him most. To other architects, the museum is, quite simply, a masterpiece. It was commissioned by wealthy patrons of the arts Kay and Velma Kimbell to house their fine collection of works of art, ranging from pre-Columbian and 7th-century Asian pieces to paintings by such towering figures of modern Western art as Cézanne, Monet, Gauguin and Picasso. It is a small building, only a storey high with a basement beneath, but it is perfect for its function, both spatially and in its wonderfully luminous natural lighting.

The basic structural element of the museum is a post-tensioned reinforced-concrete arched (or cycloid) vault, measuring 100 x 20ft (30 x 6m), and supported by columns at each corner. Walls and floors are post-tensioned two-skin and long-span structures. According to Louis Khan's engineering consultant, August Komendant, the special post-tensioning of the cycloid vaults and the post-tensioned floor and wall systems were genuine innovations to the standard way of building cycloid vaults.

The vaults are aligned in two groups, several of them being left open to form an entrance court and side passageways, with a

RIGHT & OPPOSITE: MGM Grand Hotel
Casino, Las Vegas, Nevada.

layouts and their emphasis on accessibility allied to a protected privacy.

The Atheneum Visitors Center, completed in the late 1970s, established Meier as a 'big project' architect and in the 1980s his attention increasingly turned towards designing museums at home and abroad. Among the most noteworthy of such buildings in America are the High Museum of Art in Atlanta, Georgia (page 418), that gets it undeniable impact from being based, very simply, on three cubes and a cylinder, and the coolly refined, billion-dollar Getty Center in Los Angeles (page 423).

Gambling Resort Style
Las Vegas, Nevada
1930s–present

It is the sort of image that film director David Lean would have turned into an unforgettable cinema moment: a fabulous city shimmering apparition-like on the desert horizon. But we are not in Arabia and the city is not at the heart of a stirring romance that reflects national aspirations. For this is Las Vegas, the gambling and quick-marriage capital of America, seedy and decadent to some, spectacularly exciting and dynamic to others.

However cheaply built and decorated some of Las Vegas's tourist-oriented motels, night spots and eateries may be, there is no denying that the heart of Las Vegas, along and just off the Strip, is a fabulous collection of exuberant architecture unmatched anywhere else in America – or indeed the world. For a start it boasts 16 of the world's 20 biggest resort hotels, the most luxurious of them, the Bellagio, the Mandalay Bay, the Venetian and the Paris having been built at the turn of the 20th

RIGHT & OPPOSITE: Illuminated signs,
Las Vegas, Nevada.

century. Las Vegas doesn't do history or sentiment. 'Old-fashioned' hotels, built when Ancient Egypt or Camelot, say, were the buzz themes, get bulldozed to make way for something more up-to-the-minute. The Venetian, the most spectacular hotel-casino in Las Vegas today, is built in an ultra-fashionable European style. It is a Venetian palazzo set on its own canals, complete with gondolas worked by gondoliers in striped sweaters.

In its early days, especially after a ban on gambling in Las Vegas was lifted in 1931, the place fell into the hands of mobsters from the Midwest, but things changed after the Second World War as the mobsters' hold on the town was broken. The image of Las Vegas changed, becoming more of a reflection of Main Street America taken to brash excess. This symbolism was not lost on architects. Robert Venturi (born 1925) chose to call the book on modern architectural theory that he wrote with fellow architects Denise Scott Brown (his wife) and Steven Izenour in 1971, *Learning from Las Vegas*.

The point Venturi was making was that modern architecture, while retaining its historical links, must not ignore what was actually being built on 'Main Street, U.S.A.', such as a grocery store with a Chinese restaurant on one side and a poker parlour or strip-joint on the other, none of them in the same style – or that which was being depicted in popular art such as comic strips, cartoons and advertising. Architects, according to Venturi and Scott Brown, must confront the competition from consumerism and the demands of everyday urban life. In this context, socially-aware architects should see the over-the-top hotels and garish neon signs that lit the sky above Las Vegas as

OPPOSITE and LEFT: Caesar's Palace, Las Vegas, Nevada.

OPPOSITE & LEFT: Caesar's Palace,
Las Vegas, Nevada.

Caesar's Palace and the Mirage Hotel
Casino, Las Vegas.

symbols of what Americans liked and desired and should use them as stimuli to creative thought.

Not that social awareness or the needs of the urban community is much in the minds of the designers of Las Vegas's great resort hotels. Everything is much more to do with leaving the everyday urban world behind and entering, if only for a weekend, a world of luxury.

As the web site of the mega-resort hotel, the Bellagio – the top star of Steven Soderbergh's star-laden movie *Ocean's 11* – puts it, 'Entering Bellagio, one is immediately struck by the glass ceilings admitting natural light – a rarity in Las Vegas. It illuminates the striking glamor of the surroundings and the rare and beautiful charms available for the comfort and pleasure of its guests.'

For the record, the Bellagio, named after an immensely attractive little town on Lake Como in Italy, has 3,933 rooms and 512 suites. There are 19 dining options, a 116,000-sq ft (10800-m²) casino, a 1,800-seat showroom, a night club, five swimming pools and four jacuzzis, all in Mediterranean-style settings, together with a wedding chapel offering a choice of wedding packages, an avenue of stylish shops, and various convention and meeting rooms. The inspiration for the style of the Bellagio is said to be the architecture of Tuscany, Italy.

Caesar's Palace shopping mall.

RIGHT & OPPOSITE: Las Vegas day and
night.

OPPOSITE & LEFT: Bellagio Hotel
Casino, Las Vegas.

CHAPTER EIGHT

POSTMODERNISM
from c.1960s

Lincoln Center for the Performing Arts, New York, NY

Vanna Venturi House, Philadelphia, Pennsylvania

Hyatt Regency Hotels

Best Products Showrooms: SITE designs of the 1970s

Walt Disney World, Orlando, Florida

Eaton Centre, Toronto, Ontario, Canada

AT&T Building, New York, NY

Atlantis Condominium, Miami, Florida

Roy Thomson Hall, Toronto, Ontario, Canada

High Museum of Art, Atlanta, Georgia

California Aerospace Museum, Los Angeles, California

Getty Center, Los Angeles, California

Canada Place, Vancouver, British Columbia, Canada

Walt Disney Concert Hall, Los Angeles, California

World Trade Center, New York, NY

RIGHT: Modern shingle-style house
(c.1973), Greenwich, Connecticut.
Architect: Robert Venturi.

OPPOSITE: Gordon Wu Hall,
Princetown University (1984).
Architects: Venturi/Scott Brown.

RIGHT: Edgemar Development (1987), Santa Monica, California. Architect: Frank Gehry.

OPPOSITE: Chiat Day Headquarters Building (1991), Venice, Los Angeles, California. Gehry & Associates.

For the Best Products Company, whose standard showroom was a very ordinary brick box, SITE designed in the 1970s showrooms with walls that looked as if they were peeling away from the building's framework, or walls that looked as if they were crumbling into piles of bricks. Wines and other Best architects in the 1970s, including Charles Moore and Michael Graves, were all making strong historical allusions in their buildings. Philip Johnson, in his Foreword in the catalogue of the Buildings for Best Products exhibition, mounted by the Museum of Modern Art in New York in 1979, was able to bring in references to Classical Greek temples, Michelangelo's Campidoglio (also copied a decade before in New York's Lincoln Center for the Performing Arts), 16th-century Mannerism, Expressionism and Futurism, as well as referring to 'almost antiarchitectural up-scaled sculpture', in his overview of the works in the exhibition.

Johnson ended his Foreword with: 'The Modern Movement seems really gone from the scene... Harder to define than the International Style, less arrogant and self-satisfied with their moral superiority then their ancestors, architects today are more inclusive, more permissive, more popular-oriented, indeed more popular than the Modern Movement allowed... What happens next?'

What happened next was a building that thoroughly upset the Modernist architectural establishment. This was the Public Services Building in Portland, Oregon, designed by Michael Graves (page 394). Graves had once been a white-building Modernist, and was featured, like Richard Meier, in MoMA's Five Architects exhibition of 1969. Whereas Meier remained a

RIGHT: Eaton Centre, Toronto, Canada
(1977–81). See page 412.

OPPOSITE: National Gallery of Canada,
Ottawa, Ontario, Canada (1986–88).
Architect: Moshe Safdie.

white-building man, notably in his Atheneum in Harmony, Indiana (page 371), and his Getty Center in Los Angeles (page 423), Graves changed direction, becoming one of Disney's principal architects by way of designing Best Products' showrooms.

Graves's relatively short-lived Public Services Building (it had gone by the mid-1990s) restored heavy masonry to the architectural mix, with details that looked back before Modernism to the Viennese Secession. It was also strongly coloured, with the facade of the square, 15-storey, small-windowed building being painted in yellow, brown and green in a geometrical pattern. Graves had wanted to add lots of frills in the shape of statues, swags and ribbons on marble cladding, but budget cuts ensured that none of these appeared on the final building.

By this time, other considerations had come to the fore and architects were having to work with the new technologies of a rapidly developing computer age, while at the same time thinking in terms of what was ecologically and environmentally acceptable in a world where small had become more beautiful than big.

Lincoln Center for the Performing Arts
Manhattan, New York, NY
1959–66

Modernism took a back seat as the major architectural style for important buildings in New York in the late 1950s, when work began on the Lincoln Center for the Performing Arts. Its designs and plans made it clear that this was going to be a spectacularly formal and Classical complex.

Planned as the city's most important cultural area, the Lincoln Center eventually covered some 15 acres (6 hectares) of the former Upper West Side slums that Leonard Bernstein had used as the setting for his classic musical/opera, *West Side Story*. It was entirely appropriate, then, that when the first sod of earth on the site was turned by President Eisenhower in 1959, Leonard Bernstein should have been on hand to conduct the New York Philharmonic Orchestra and the Juilliard Choir in a rousing performance of Handel's 'Halleluja' chorus.

Some of the biggest names in American architecture – Max Abramovitz, Wallace K. Harrison, Philip Johnson and Eero Saarinen – were involved in designing the buildings and surroundings of the Lincoln Center. The plaza was laid out by Wallace Harrison (1895–1981), a Beaux-Arts-trained architect and planner, whose previous work in New York had included the Rockefeller Center and the United Nations Building. He also designed the arcaded opera house while his partner, Max Abramovitz (1908–76), who has also had a Beaux-Arts training, designed the Philharmonic Hall. Philip Johnson (1906–2005) took on the theatre in the complex.

By 1966, the Center's three main buildings, the New York

RIGHT: Lincoln Center for the
Performing Arts, Manhattan, New York.

OPPOSITE: Vanna Venturi House,
Chestnut Hill, Philadelphia,
Pennsylvania (1964). Architect: Robert
Venturi.

Philharmonic Concert Hall (opened in 1962), the New York
State Theater (1964) and the Metropolitan Opera House (1966),
were complete. They were grouped around Harrison's
spectacular plaza, the design of which was clearly based on the
piazza that Michelangelo designed for the Campidoglio on the
Capitoline Hill in Rome four centuries before. The fountain in
the centre of the plaza was designed by Philip Johnson and there
was also a sculptural work – Henry Moore's 'Reclining Figure'.

Rather out of place in its setting among Manhattan's great
commercial skyscrapers, the coolly Classical Lincoln Center for
the Performing Arts hinted at the possibility of a post-Mies van
der Rohe world of architecture, although perhaps not in the
style that at least two of its designers envisaged. Postmodernism
may have rejected Mies's 'less is more', but by the time the first
stage of the Lincoln Center was completed, Robert Venturi has
published his influential *Complexity and Contradiction in
Architecture* and architecture was clearly not going to be
returning to Classical formalism.

Vanna Venturi House
Chestnut Hill, Philadelphia, Pennsylvania
1964

Robert Venturi (born Philadelphia 1925) designed this small
house for his mother in a spirit of 'less is a bore' anti-
Modernism. His seminal book, *Complexity and Contradiction in
Architecture*, in which he analyzed Western architecture in terms
of its contradictions and multi-layered meanings, was just a
couple of years from publication and Venturi would have been
deep in the throes of writing it while he was designing the house.

applied to just about every building in Walt Disney World and could be said to define the unique Disney style in a way that neither 'Modernist' nor 'Postmodernist' quite manage to do.

Disney chooses its accommodation styles with great care. Nothing is ever just an ordinary-looking hotel, motel or camp; it will always have a recognizable style, be it Eastern Seaboard Resort, South-Western U.S. Mexican, New Orleans French Quarter, or Twentieth-Century Pop. You'd expect a de luxe hotel like the 1,008-room Contemporary, in the Magic Kingdom area, to be stylish, but its 'Retro-futuristic' design is jaw-dropping. From the moment the monorail train disappears into its enormous A-frame tower and stops in the lobby, with its tiers of balconies and 90-ft (27-m)-high mural, visitors know they are somewhere special.

Then there is the Grand Floridian, which out-Flaglers Henry Flagler's great Florida hotels of the turn of the century. The Grand Floridian is an 867-room Victorian stately home, complete with gabled and shingled roofs, turrets and towers, carved mouldings, balustrades and verandas, with ceiling fans and intricate latticework. Inside the main building, the Grand Lobby soars five storeys to a ceiling that is a riot of stained-glass domes and glittering chandeliers. This turn-of-the-century theme extends to the costumes worn by the staff, to shop displays, room décor and restaurant design.

Walt Disney World celebrates in inimitable Disney style in the architecture of four centuries of American history. No doubt the grandchildren and great-grandchildren of today's visitors will be able to experience a fifth century of American architecture according to Disney.

POSTMODERNISM FROM c.1960s

OPPOSITE: Eaton Centre, Toronto, Canada. Architect: Eberhard Zeidler.

Eaton Centre
Toronto, Ontario, Canada
1977–81

Eberhard Zeidler was born in Germany in 1926, where he studied architecture before emigrating to Canada in 1951. After working as a partner in two architectural practices, one in Peterborough, Ontario, the other in Hamilton, Zeidler formed the Zeidler Roberts Partnership in Toronto, which eventually acquired offices in Washington, Florida, London (England), and Berlin.

A major project for Zeidler's Hamilton partnership at the end of the 1960s was the McMaster University Health Sciences Centre in Hamilton, Ontario (1967–72), the first integrated patient-care, educational and research complex in the world, and a considerable advance on Louis Khan's Salk Institute in La Jolla, California. To turn from this to designing a shopping centre for downtown Toronto must have sounded like a pleasantly relaxing diversion for the Zeidler Roberts partnership. In fact, the Eaton Centre was just as revolutionary and just as successful as the McMaster Centre, and it was the multi-prize-winning Eaton Centre, rather than the McMaster project, that made Zeidler famous in Canada.

In Zeidler's hands, the Eaton Centre was rather more than just another off-street shopping mall, shoddily designed and hastily thrown up. For a start, he had a very large site at his disposal. Timothy Eaton had founded a dry goods store on Yonge Street, Toronto, in the 19th century that was to be the first shop in what by the end of the century had become Canada's largest chain of department stores. The site of the first shop had spread to cover a large area bounded by four main streets in the heart of Toronto, which the Eaton family wanted to redevelop to include office as well as retail buildings.

Zeidler, who worked in conjunction with Bregman & Hamann Architects on the project, seems to have been inspired by Eaton's early history to look back to 19th-century European architecture when he planned the new centre. The handsome, glass-roofed Eaton Centre seems to have been designed on the lines of the world's first all glass large public building, Joseph Paxton's Crystal Palace, built for the Great Exhibition of 1851, while the Galleria Vittorio Emanuele II in Milan, Italy, was certainly another model.

When the first phase of the complex opened in 1977, the people of Toronto, which is a city where winters are long and bitterly cold, found that Zeidler had given them an indoor, multi-levelled, vaulted glass-ceilinged shopping galleria, with more than 300 stores in a mega-size glasshouse covering 1,000,000sq ft (93000m²). Dozens of trees and plants gave the centre a feeling of being in a garden, enhanced by fountains and 'outdoor' cafes, and with natural lighting. From the ceiling hung a group of fibreglass Canada geese, the work of artist Michael Snow.

Two years later, the second phase of the development, a second store plus an 18-screen cinema complex, opened, while between 1977 and 1992 three office skyscrapers were built on the site. The Eaton Centre was enormously successful. It was a very novel approach to shopping-mall construction, and apart from anything else, was one of the first downtown shopping malls in North America, which the people of Toronto adopted with great pleasure from the day it first opened for business. It was also very profitable and is credited with keeping the whole Eaton chain

RIGHT & OPPOSITE: Eaton Centre,
Toronto, Canada.

AT&T Building, Manhattan, New York.
Architect: Philip Johnson.

afloat for two decades before it went bankrupt in 1999. The splendid Eaton Centre shopping space is now occupied by Sears Canada, which has retained the Eaton name, perhaps in tribute to Timothy Eaton and the small shop he opened so long ago in the heart of Toronto.

AT&T Building
Manhattan, New York, NY
1978–82

When the great communications corporation AT&T decided to move out of its old headquarters on Broadway in New York's financial district, it chose Philip Johnson to design its new building on Madison Avenue. Working in association with John Burgee, Johnson came up with the most discussed building of the 1980s, a flagship Postmodernist building so controversial that it made the cover of *Time* magazine. It still divides critics to this day, even though some of its undeniably poor features, such as the windy, sunless open arcades 60ft (18m) above ground level, and the galleria behind the building that behaved like a wind-tunnel, were made good within ten years of its completion.

AT&T is said to have wanted its new headquarters building to be as direct a statement as a Norman Rockwell painting. Philip Johnson certainly provided that, in a formal high-rise building that looked back to Louis Sullivan's 'base, shaft and capital' design formula. Johnson's 647-ft (197-m) AT&T Building has a strong vertical emphasis and is clad in 132,000 metric tonnes of pink granite. Above its ground-floor base, with its stone piers and huge arched entrance portal, rises a column comprising 28 floors of identical offices (designed to house

1,500 employees), topped by an extraordinary pediment with an exploded gable split by a 345-ft (105-m) wide circular break (described on the plans as a 'round oculus'). This last feature very soon came to be called a 'Chippendale' top, after the great 18th-century English furniture designer.

Johnson continued his Postmodernist take on older styles in the ground-floor public lobby. Behind the entrance arch sits a colossal gilded statue of Commerce, removed from the roof of the old AT&T building and reinstalled in a Romanesque style setting with Postmodern touches.

Was Philip Johnson having fun when he designed the AT&T Building? Had he really intended to make it look like the back of a Chippendale chair? Now he was certainly 'decorating the box', as several critics remarked. But was it a 'harbinger of a new era' as one critic described it, or was it, in the words of another, a piece of 'social and political neoconservatism'? Today, a quarter of a century after its completion, the AT&T is generally considered to be a failure as a modern urban building. 'Misconceived', 'undignified', 'unsuitable for its site', 'inhospitable' and 'a compositional failure' are a few of the criticisms levelled at it in the past that were not totally negated by the major renovations carried out by its new occupiers, the Sony Corporation, in the 1990s.

Atlantis Condominium
Miami, Florida
1979–82

The problem of how to use urban space with maximum effectiveness, while avoiding the boring high-rise box that was unlikely to attract future capital investment, was given many different solutions by America's Postmodernist architects and designers. Not too many were as glamorous – or became as famous (because of its presence in the opening shots of the TV series, *Miami Vice*) – as the Atlantis Condominium. This 18-storey luxury apartment block was designed by the Florida-based partnership of Arquitectonica, led by Bernardo Fort-Brescia (born 1950) and Laurinda Spear (born 1951).

The Atlantis was built on the edge of Biscayne Bay on land that had once been a private estate, its original mansion having been restored as a clubhouse. Basically a standard apartment block, the dictates of local building regulations meant the Atlantis had to be designed as a narrow slab and its materials – reinforced concrete columns and concrete slabs – were not the most exciting. What gave the Atlantis style and glamour was the way in which its design had been so well conceived by its young architects.

The glass-covered north facade of the building has a reflective glass covering and is surmounted by a 24-ft (7-m) vivid red triangle. Four bright-yellow triangles extend from the lower levels of the facade, and an immense 37-ft (11-m) square section has been cut out of the middle of the building. The gap that remains, which the architects called a 'sky court', is painted bright yellow and has a red spiral staircase running up one side of it and a red balcony projecting from the other, while between them a green palm tree bobs and sways in the breeze. Crockett and Tubbs, speeding past in their flashy police limo, could not have failed to notice the Atlantis.

The building's south side, facing Key Biscayne, is just as

OPPOSITE: Roy Thomson Hall, Toronto, Ontario, Canada. Architect: Arthur Erickson.

exuberantly designed: a royal blue grid frames a series of balconies, its line broken only by that bright-yellow sky court and the red triangle on the roof. At its base is a white cube, set at an angle as if the section cut out of the facade has been left to lie where it fell. The cube contains a health club.

The Atlantis's style – a purist, oversized mix of geometric shapes strikingly coloured – was largely the work of Laurinda Spear, one of the most prolific women architects in America since Julia Morgan, favourite architect of William Randolph Hearst. It has become Arquitectonica's trademark style, much in demand in Miami and beyond, and copies of it are to be found as far away as China, though it could be that the *Miami Vice* connection has been at work.

Roy Thomson Hall
Toronto, Ontario, Canada
1982

Toronto-born Roy Thomson was one of Canada's most famous exports in the mid 20th century. He was a newspaper magnate who founded a publishing empire in Britain and became a peer, the 1st Baron Thomson of Fleet. It is not surprising, then, that Toronto should have chosen in the 1980s to name the city's new concert hall after him. Nor is it surprising that for such a prestige project Toronto should have called in one of Canada's best-known architects, Arthur Erickson (born in Vancouver, 1924), to design it.

Erickson had spent much of the 1970s designing and overseeing the construction of Vancouver's huge Robson Square and Provincial Law Courts civic centre complex and was consequently well aware of the contribution that well-designed civic amenities could make to the life of a city. Working with the architects Mather and Haldenby, Erickson gave Toronto a glass-sheathed concert hall with a sloping curvilinear shape resembling a large inverted bowl. When it is lit from inside at night, the hall appears transparent, while in daylight, the diamond-shaped panels of the glass exterior shimmer, reflecting the blue of the sky.

Inside, the 2,812-seat auditorium is renowned for its excellent acoustics. It is actually in a 'sound lock', made by insulating it inside a thick circular passageway with entry doors at intervals. The fabrics for the seats, carpets and ceiling decorations were all chosen for their acoustics-enhancing qualities and woven, tubular hanging banners can be raised or lowered to achieve changes in resonance. Dominating the auditorium ceiling is a centrepiece formed as an illuminated double-ringed oculus; a shower of suspended metal 'raindrops' lights the stage.

Today, the recently renovated hall is home to the Toronto Symphony Orchestra and the Toronto Mendelssohn Choir. It is also one of the main venues for the annual Toronto International Film Festival. As Arthur Erickson intended, the Roy Thomson Hall makes a continuing great contribution to the life of Toronto.

High Museum of Art
Atlanta, Georgia
1983

The New York architect Richard Meier (b. 1934) was a member of the 'New York Five' who gained prominence through an exhibition at the Museum of Modern Art in 1969, another member being the future Disney architect Michael Graves. All

Walt Disney Concert Hall
Los Angeles, California
1988–2003

Now nearly 80, Frank Gehry is one of the world's star architects, so famous that he has had a starring role in *The Simpsons* (designing Springfield's concert hall) and is in demand all over the world for public buildings, particularly museums. But it is for Los Angeles, a city that regards him as its favourite adopted son, that Frank Gehry has produced much of his recent work.

Gehry's latest contribution to the architecture of Los Angeles is the Walt Disney Concert Hall, the fourth venue to be built in the Los Angeles Music Center, and its undoubted visual highlight. Gehry was comissioned in 1988 to design this project, funded by the Disney family, planned to be a 'living room for the city'. Although his designs were unveiled in 1991 and work got under way on a six-level subterranean parking garage for the complex in 1992, it was not until 1999 that work began on the concert hall itself. The 1990s was a decade of earthquakes, race riots and global recession for Los Angeles, making funding for the project slow to materialize. Eventually, the Disney family's contribution to the project reached over $100 million, the County of Los Angeles provided the land and also funded the parking garage, and many more corporations, foundations and individuals in Los Angeles and California also gave generous donations.

The curving, stainless steel and titanium-panelled Walt Disney Concert Hall complex, set on three-and-a-half acres of central Los Angeles, eventually opened to worldwide acclaim in 2003. If it had been completed when originally planned, it would have opened before Gehry's hugely celebrated Guggenheim Museum in Bilboa and it, rather than the Bilbao museum, would have become the archetype for urban renewal architecture.

In the long run, however, these things do not matter much. Los Angeles has given itself one of the finest concert halls in the world and an internationally recognized architectural landmark. The Walt Disney Concert Hall is the home of the Los Angeles Philharmonic, which, courtesy of Frank Gehry, has in its hardwood-panelled main auditorium one of the world's most acoustically sophisticated spaces in which to work.

And there is more Gehry to come. Early in 2006, Los Angeles heard that it is to get two more buildings alongside the concert hall, both designed by 'the world's foremost trophy architect', as Gehry was recently described. This time, the buildings are to be L-shaped towers, one 47-storeys-high, the other 24. Completion is set for 2009 for these first buildings in a massive redevelopment of Los Angeles' downtown hinterland.

World Trade Center
Manhattan, New York, NY
2001–c.2012

The first date given here for the rebuilding of the World Trade Center site, where the Twin Towers had been an essential part of New York's skyline since 1973, reflects the fact that within days of the terrible events of 11 September 2001, the city of New York was discussing how those who lost their lives could best be remembered and how the destroyed buildings would be replaced.

POSTMODERNISM FROM c.1960s

The competition to decide the shape of the new World Trade Center was won in 2003 by Daniel Libeskind, born in Poland in 1946, who became a U.S. citizen in 1965 and was best-known at the time for his acclaimed Jewish Museum in Berlin (2001). Libeskind's master plan for the site includes two large public spaces, the Park of Heroes and the wonderfully visionary Wedge of Light in honour of the victims. The extremely precise engineering incorporated in the latter will enable the sun to shine without a shadow every year on 11 September, between the hours of 8.46 a.m., when the first plane struck, and 10.28 a.m., when the second tower collapsed. Libeskind's master plan also envisages five towers, including the Freedom Tower, and a memorial and museum.

The construction of the Freedom Tower, a controversial design by David Childs, was delayed by argument for years, largely because of its soaring height, which at 1,776-ft (541m) would make it the tallest structure in the world, and which some regarded as both hubristic and unsafe. After a breakthrough deal was made between city planners and Larry Silverstein, holder of the lease on the site, construction began on the Freedom Tower in May 2006, two months after work had started on Michael Arad's World Trade Center Memorial (Reflecting Absence) and museum, which are expected to be completed by 2009.

All five skyscrapers planned for the 16-acre (6.5-hectare) site are due to be completed by 2012. Two British architects have each won a tower. Lord Rogers of Riverside, designer of the Pompidou Centre in Paris and the Millennium Dome in London will design Tower 2, an office tower, while Lord Foster of Thames Bank, designer of the Berlin Reichstag building and the controversial Swiss Re building, usually called the Gherkin, in London, is the designer of Tower 3, also an office skyscraper. The Japanese architect Fumihiko Maki, whose design for a new United Nations building in New York has caused another architectural controversy in the city, will design Tower 4. The final skyscraper, Tower 5, which was to have been designed by Jean Nouvel, of France, has been taken over by the New York Port Authority and will probably be developed for residential use.

INDEX

PHOTOGRAPHIC ACKNOWLEDGEMENTS

Photographic Acknowledgements

AA Photo Library: page 287 right, 289, 290, 291 left, 292 left, 299, 300

© Angelo Hornak/Corbis: pages 348 right, 351

© Bettman/Corbis: page 209

© Corbis: page 251

© David Sailors/Corbis: page 324

© Earl & Nazima Rowall/Corbis: page: 59

© Farrell Grehan/Corbis pages: 36, 433

© G. E. Kidder Smith/Corbis: page 49

© Jeremy Horner/Corbis: page 350

© Joseph Sohm; ChromoSohm Inc./Corbis: page 424

© Joseph Sohm, Visions of America/Corbis: page 327

© Kelly-Mooney Photography/Corbis: page 337

© Kevin Flemming/Corbis: page 420

© Lee Snider/Corbis: pages 66, 74, 150

© Richard Schulman/Corbis: page 322

© Robert Holmes/Corbis: pages 70, 356

© Roger Kessmeyer/Corbis: page 422

© Royalty-Free/Corbis: page 136

© Rudy Sulgan/Corbis: page 236

© Vince Streano/Corbis: page 285

Edifice © page 106

Edifice © Andrian Forty: page 393

Edifice © Gillian Darley: pages 68, 114, 140, 348, 369

Edifice © Kim Sayer: pages 87, 391 right, 392, 405

Edifice © Lewis/Darley: pages 84, 113, 120, 121

Edifice © Paula Weideger: page 174

Edifice © Philippa Lewis: pages 14, 15, 18, 147

Edifice © T. Brubaker: page 335

Library of Congress: pages 28 left, 35, 38, 50, 54, 55, 118, 119, 148, 192 both, 202 both, 211, 214, 217 left, 235, 244, 431

© 2006 Thomas A. Heinz: pages 20, 115, 117, 163, 164, 165, 203, 204, 206 both, 207, 208, 212, 216, 217 right, 218, 219 both, 220, 221, 222, 223, 224, 226 both, 227, 229 both, 230, 231, 232 both, 233, 234 both, 238 both, 240, 241, 242 both, 243, 245, 246, 247, 264, 265 both, 278, 280, 301, 302, 303, 305 both, 306, 307, 309, 310 both, 315, 316, 318, 320, 321, 329, 331, 332, 333, 343, 345, 346, 347, 353, 354, 357, 358, 362, 366, 367, 407

Art Directors & TRIP Photo Library/the following photographers:

Adina Tovy: pages 11, 16, 23, 29, 64, 97, 98, 131, 143, 152, 153, 154, 156, 194, 197, 257, 259, 376, 377

Allan Wright: page 272

Alex Bartel: page 355 right

Amanda Edwards: pages 99, 253, 255, 267, 293, 379, 386, 396

Amer Ghazzal: page 142

Anne-Marie Bazalik: page 298

Brian Vikander: pages 8, 85

Bob Turner: pages 77, 104, 105, 107, 129, 134, 256 right, 334, 398, 399, 411, 413, 414, 415, 419

Chris Rennie: pages 13 left, 60, 161, 200

Chris Ryan: page 63

Colin Conway: page 33, 95, 124

Constance Toms: pages 53, 390

Derick Mcgroarty: pages 17, 94

Douglas Houghton: page 122

Earl Young: pages 79, 173, 188, 189, 193, 196, 325, 326, 356, 374 left

George Taylor: page 355 right

Giles Strokoe: page 102, 116

Helene Rogers: page 3, 4, 21 left, 81, 144, 183, 215, 239, 288, 400, 401, 402, 403, 404, 409, 410

Ian Mitchell: page 65

Jack Stanely: page 391 left

Jane Sweeney: pages 389, 426, 428

Jan Isachsen: pages 42, 43, 90, 125, 395

Jan Roberts: pages 31, 32, 57,

Jeff Greenberg: pages 5, 13 right, 24, 28 right, 58, 76, 91, 92, 93, 101, 187, 254, 261, 295 both

Jerry Dennis: pages 39, 40, 312 right, 313, 373

Keith Cardwell: page 10, 34

Ken Mclaren: pages 12 right, 44, 138, 146, 260

Laura Gayler: pages 372, 378, 383

Linda Sole: pages 111, 213, 249 left, 250

Malcolm Lee: pages 128, 158, 287 left, 296

Malcolm Jenkin: page 375

Martin Barlow: pages 30 both, 71, 72, 127, 130, 157, 176, 177, 178, 179, 180, 249 right, 281, 282, 283 right, 312 left, 338, 339, 394, 397, 429 left

Maxwell Mackenzie: page 416

Mel Longhurst: page 26, 46

Mike Peters: page 291 right

Nick Wiseman: page 2

Peter Treanor: pages 112, 283 left, 294, 374 right, 380, 382

Robin Belin: page 361

Robin Smith: pages 169, 268, 269, 270, 271, 384, 387

Roy Styles: pages 132, 170, 172

Sergio Dorantes: pages 12 left, 190

Spencer Grant: pages 19, 27, 47, 62, 83, 88, 89, 96, 100, 109, 123, 160, 162, 195, 256 left, 274, 292 right, 311, 330, 385

Stuart Haden: pages 25, 75

Terry Why: pages 110, 297

Tibor Bognar: pages 6, 7, 21 right, 61, 108, 133, 135, 151, 155, 166, 167, 168, 185, 198, 201, 336, 364, 381, 427

Tony Freeman: page 80

Warren Jacobs: page 429

Van Greaves: page 387

Viesti Associates: pages 137, 276, 423

FRONT COVER
Above left: Jeff Greenberg
Above right: Spencer Grant
Below left: Robin Smith
Below right: Brian Vikander

BACK COVER
Robin Smith